simple
potatoes
& rice
step-by-step

THUNDER BAY
P · R · E · S · S

San Diego, California

Thunder Bay Press
An imprint of the Advantage Publishers Group
THUNDER BAY 5880 Oberlin Drive, San Diego, CA 92121-4794
P·R·E·S·S www.advantagebooksonline.com

All notations of errors or omissions should be addressed to Thunder Bay Press, editorial department, at the above address. All other correspondence (author inquiries, permissions) concerning the content of this book should be addressed to The Foundry Creative Media Company Limited, Crabtree Hall, Crabtree Lane, Fulham, London, SW6 6TY, England.

ISBN 1-57145-747-X

Library of Congress Cataloging-in-Publication Data available upon request.

Printed in Korea.

1 2 3 4 5   06 05 04 03 02

ACKNOWLEDGMENTS

Authors: Catherine Atkinson, Juliet Barker, Gina Steer, Vicki Smallwood, Carol Tennant, Mari Mererid Williams, and Elizabeth Wolf-Cohen
Editorial Consultant: Gina Steer
Project Editor: Karen Fitzpatrick
Photography: Colin Bowling, Paul Forrester, and Stephen Brayne
Home Economists and Stylists: Jacqueline Bellefontaine, Mandy Phipps, Vicki Smallwood, and Penny Stephens
Design Team: Helen Courtney, Jennifer Bishop, Lucy Bradbury, and Chris Herbert

All props supplied by Barbara Stewart at Surfaces

NOTE
Recipes using uncooked eggs should be avoided by infants, the elderly, pregnant women, and anyone with a compromised immune system.

Special thanks to everyone involved in this book, particularly Karen Fitzpatrick and Gina Steer.

CONTENTS

SOUPS & STARTERS

FISH

MEAT

POULTRY

VEGETABLES

ENTERTAINING

CLEANLINESS IN THE KITCHEN

It is well worth remembering that many foods can carry some form of bacteria. In most cases, the worst it will lead to is a bout of food poisoning or gastroenteritis, although for certain people this can be more serious—the risk can be reduced or eliminated by good food hygiene and proper cooking.

Do not buy food that is past its sell-by date and do not consume any food that is past its use-by date. When buying food, use your eyes and nose. If the food looks tired, limp, has a bad color, and/or a rank, acrid, or simply bad smell, do not buy or eat it under any circumstances.

Do take special care when preparing raw meat and fish. A separate chopping board should be used for each; wash the knife, board, and your hands thoroughly before handling or preparing any other food.

Regularly clean, defrost, and clear out the refrigerator or freezer—it is worth checking the packaging to see exactly how long each product is safe to freeze.

Avoid handling food if suffering from an upset stomach, as bacteria can be passed through food preparation.

Dishtowels must be washed and changed regularly. Ideally, use paper towels, which can be thrown out after use. More durable cloths should be left to soak in bleach, then washed in the washing machine in hot water.

Keep your hands, cooking utensils, and food preparation surfaces clean and do not allow pets to climb onto any work surfaces.

BUYING

Avoid bulk buying where possible, especially fresh produce such as meat, poultry, fish, fruits, and vegetables, unless buying to store in the freezer. Fresh foods lose their nutritional value rapidly, so buying a little at a time minimizes loss of nutrients. It also eliminates a packed refrigerator that can reduce the effectiveness of the refrigeration process.

When buying prepackaged goods, such as cream and yogurt, check that the packaging is intact and not damaged or pierced. Cans should not be dented, pierced, or rusty. Check the sell-by dates even for cans and packages of dry ingredients, such as flour and rice. Store fresh foods in the refrigerator as soon as possible—not in the car or the office.

When buying frozen foods, ensure that they are not heavily iced on the outside and the contents feel completely frozen. Ensure that the frozen foods have been stored at a temperature below 0° F. Place in the freezer as soon as possible after purchase.

PREPARATION

Make sure that all work surfaces and utensils are clean and dry. Hygiene should be given priority at all times.

Separate chopping boards should be used for raw and cooked meats, fish, and vegetables. Currently, a variety of good-quality plastic boards come in various designs and colors. This makes differentiating easier, and the plastic has the added hygienic advantage of being washable at high temperatures in the dishwasher. If using the board for fish, first wash in cold water, then in hot to prevent odor. Also, remember that knives and utensils should always be thoroughly cleaned after use.

When cooking, be particularly careful to keep cooked and raw food separate to avoid any contamination. It is worth washing all fruits and vegetables regardless of whether they are going to be eaten raw or lightly cooked. This rule should apply even to prewashed herbs and salads.

Do not reheat food more than once. If using a microwave, always check that the food is piping hot all the way through. (In theory, the food should reach 160° F and needs to be cooked at that temperature for at least three minutes to ensure that all bacteria are killed.)

All frozen poultry must be thoroughly thawed before using. Remove the food to be thawed from the freezer and place in a shallow dish to contain the juices. Leave the food in the refrigerator until it is completely thawed. A 3-lb. whole chicken will take about 26 to 30 hours to thaw. To speed up the process, immerse the chicken in cold water. However, make sure that the water is changed regularly. When the joints can move freely and no ice crystals remain in the cavity, the bird is completely thawed.

Once thawed, pat the chicken dry. Place the chicken in a shallow dish, cover lightly, and store as close to the base of the refrigerator as possible. The chicken should be cooked as soon as possible.

Some foods can be cooked from frozen, including many

prepackaged foods, such as soups, sauces, casseroles, and breads. Where applicable, follow the manufacturers' instructions.

Vegetables and fruits can also be cooked from frozen, but meats and fish should be thawed first. The only time food can be refrozen is when the food has been thoroughly thawed, then cooked. Once the food has cooled, it can be frozen again. On such occasions the food can only be stored for one month.

All poultry and game (except for duck) must be cooked thoroughly. When cooked, the juices will run clear from the thickest part of the bird—the best area to try is usually the thigh. Other meats, like ground meat and pork, should be cooked all the way through. Fish should turn opaque, be firm in texture, and break easily into large flakes.

When cooking leftovers, make sure they are reheated until piping hot and that any sauce or soup reaches the boiling point before eating.

STORING

REFRIGERATING AND FREEZING

Meat, poultry, fish, seafood, and dairy products should all be refrigerated. The temperature of the refrigerator should be between 34 to 41° F, while the freezer temperature should not rise above 0° F.

To ensure the optimum refrigerator and freezer temperature, avoid leaving the door open. Try not to overstock the refrigerator, as this reduces the airflow inside and reduces its effectiveness in cooling the food within.

When refrigerating cooked food, allow it to cool down quickly and completely before refrigerating. Hot food will raise the temperature of the refrigerator and possibly affect, or spoil, other food stored in it.

Food within the refrigerator and freezer should always be covered. Raw and cooked food should be stored in separate parts of the refrigerator. Cooked food should be kept on the top shelves of the refrigerator, while raw meat, poultry, and fish should be placed on bottom shelves to avoid drips and cross-contamination. It is recommended that eggs should be refrigerated in order to maintain their freshness and shelf life.

Take care that frozen foods are not stored in the freezer for too long. Blanched vegetables can be stored for one month; beef, lamb, poultry, and pork for six months; and unblanched vegetables and fruits in syrup for a year. Oily fish and sausages can be stored for three months. Dairy products can last four to six months, while cakes and pastries can be kept for three to six months.

HIGH-RISK FOODS

Certain foods may carry risks to people who are considered vulnerable, such as the elderly, the ill, pregnant women, babies, young infants, and those with a compromised immune system.

It is advisable to avoid those foods listed below which belong in a higher-risk category.

There is a slight chance that some eggs carry salmonella. Cook the eggs until both the yolk and the white are firm to eliminate this risk. Pay particular attention to dishes and products incorporating lightly cooked or raw eggs, which should be eliminated from the diet. Sauces, including hollandaise and mayonnaise, mousses, soufflés, and meringues all use raw or lightly cooked eggs, as do custard-based dishes, ice creams, and sorbets. These are all considered high-risk foods to the vulnerable groups mentioned above.

Certain meats and poultry also carry the potential risk of salmonella and so should be cooked thoroughly until the juices run clear and there is no pinkness left. Unpasteurized products such as milk, cheese (especially soft cheese), pâté, and meat (both raw and cooked) all have the potential risk of listeria and should be avoided.

When buying seafood, buy from a reputable source that has a high turnover to ensure freshness. Fish should have bright, clear eyes, shiny skin, and bright pink or red gills. The fish should feel stiff to the touch, with a slight smell of sea air and iodine. The flesh of fish steaks and fillets should be translucent with no signs of discoloration. Mollusks, such as scallops, clams, and mussels, are sold fresh and are still alive. Avoid any that are open or do not close when tapped lightly. In the same way, univalves should withdraw back into their shells when lightly prodded. When choosing cephalopods, such as squid and octopus, look for a firm flesh and pleasant sea smell.

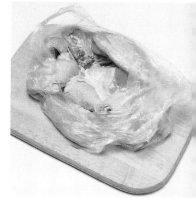

As with all fish, including shellfish, care is required when freezing. It is imperative to check whether the fish has been frozen before. If it has been frozen, then it should not be frozen again under any circumstances.

VARIETIES OF POTATOES AND STORAGE

The humble potato is generally taken for granted, and the versatility and huge number of varieties of this delicious vegetable are often forgotten. Worldwide there are thousands of different types of potatoes and for about two thirds of the world, they are the staple food. In the U.S., almost three quarters of main crop potatoes are made up of just five varieties. Consumers, however, have gradually become more demanding, so a wider range of potatoes suitable for different uses is now available. Although you will still find bags simply labeled "red" and "white" in supermarkets, alongside them is also a selection of named varieties. Many of the old varieties of potato are currently being revived, as well as new ones being created.

Potatoes are classified according to how early in the season they are ready for harvesting and are named as follows: first early, second early, and main crop. The first earlies are the first new potatoes on the market; they are very fresh and young, and the skins can simply be rubbed off. The second earlies are still new potatoes, but their skins will have begun to set. These potatoes will be difficult to scrape and are better cooked in their skins. Main crop potatoes are available all year round and may have been stored for several months. Individual potato varieties have their own characteristics. Some main crop varieties are better for boiling than baking and vice versa, so choose the most appropriate type of potato for the dish being prepared. The list below describes different varieties of potatoes and their uses.

AILSA These medium-sized potatoes are round or oval, with white skins and creamy-colored, floury flesh. Ailsa potatoes are excellent for boiling and for making french fries.

ALL-BLUE These soft, moist potatoes have a distinct deep-blue skin and flesh. They have an outstanding flavor and a moist texture. All-blue potatoes are ideal for baking or boiling and can be used in salads.

ARRAN COMET These round, and sometimes oval, new potatoes have a white skin and creamy flesh. Large ones are good for making french fries.

ARRAN PILOT The firm flesh of these potatoes makes them an ideal choice for salads. They have white flesh and skins.

ARRAN VICTORY These oval-shaped potatoes have a deep-purple skin and a bright, white flesh. They are the oldest variety of Arran potatoes still available. Arran Victory potatoes have a very floury texture and flavor, and are excellent for baking and boiling. Currently they are undergoing a revival—it is well worth seeking this variety out.

ASPERGE Also known as la ratte and cornichon, these potatoes have a yellow skin and a creamy, very waxy flesh. They are good steamed or boiled and are perfect for salads.

BELLE DE FONTENA These long potatoes often have a curved shape. Their skins are pale-yellow, and their flesh is firm, waxy, and yellow. Belle de Fontena have a wonderful buttery flavor and are particularly good boiled, in salads, or mashed.

CARIBÉ These potatoes are fairly dry and have a purple skin. The flesh is snow-white in color and has a waxy texture. Caribé are good all-around potatoes.

CATRIONA These kidney-shaped potatoes with purple markings around the eyes on the skin and a pale-yellow flesh have a delicious flavor and are ideal for baking, boiling, and mashing.

CHARLOTTE These oval or pear-shaped potatoes with pale-yellow skin and flesh, a firm, waxy texture, and a flavor not unlike chestnuts are particularly good boiled, steamed, and in salads, but can also be baked.

CLEOPATRA These oval new potatoes are suitable for boiling, have pink or red skin, and a light-yellow, dense flesh.

COLMO Medium, round, or oval, these potatoes have a white skin and golden, firm flesh. Their texture and color make them particularly good for mashing.

DESIRÉE Probably the world's most popular red-skinned potatoes with pale-yellow flesh, a firm texture, and good flavor. These potatoes are good all-arounders and are great for both mashing and roasting. They also hold their shape well enough for boiling.

DIAMONT These potatoes were a common and popular variety in the 1930s and are still available now. They are long and oval shaped, with a rough, white skin, and a firm, waxy yellow interior. Their flavor is slightly sharp and nutty.

DUKE OF YORK These long, oval, new potatoes have a sweet flavor, firm texture, pale creamy-colored skins, and light-yellow flesh. A red-skinned variety is also available.

EPICURE Round potatoes with white, or sometimes pink-tinged skin, creamy, firm flesh, and a distinctive flavor. Suitable for both boiling and baking.

FINGERLING There are three varieties of fingerling potatoes. Swedish Peanut fingerlings have a dry texture, making them good for mashed potatoes. Use Rosefinn Apple fingerlings for baking, or boiling, and for salads, it is best to use Russian Banana fingerlings.

GOLDEN WONDER These large, oval potatoes have a dark, russet-colored skin and light yellow flesh. They are excellent for baking and their floury texture makes them especially good for french fries.

HOME GUARD Round or slightly oval, with white skins and creamy-colored flesh, these potatoes have a dry, floury texture and a good flavor, with slightly bitter overtones. These potatoes are ideal for boiling, roasting, and making french fries. They were a favorite during the Second World War and are one of the first varieties of new potatoes available.

IDAHO (RUSSET) Also known as russet Burbank, these potatoes have a brown, rough skin, and are long, with a slightly rounded shape. The flesh has a dry texture, and they are high in starch making them great for baking. They are also excellent for making french fries.

KERR'S PINK Round, pink-skinned potatoes with creamy-white flesh and a floury texture. These potatoes are suitable for boiling, baking, mashing, roasting, and making french fries.

KING EDWARD These large white-skinned potatoes are among the best known and most popular. They have creamy-colored, very floury flesh and are good all-arounders. They are particularly suited to roasting and baking, but are not so good for salads.

MARFONA These are good baking potatoes, also suitable for boiling, but not for roasting.

MARIS BARD These white-skinned potatoes have firm, waxy flesh, with a slightly earthy taste. They are good for boiling and suitable for most other methods. They should be avoided, however, late in the season when they lose their flavor and often disintegrate during cooking.

MARIS PEER These potatoes have white flesh and skin, with an excellent flavor. They are good for salads, as well as boiling and steaming.

MORAG These potatoes have a pale skin and a white, waxy flesh. Serve them boiled, steamed, or baked.

NADINE These potatoes are available in two sizes. There are the small new potatoes and the slightly larger-sized potatoes, which are suitable for baking. Nadine potatoes have creamy-yellow skins and white, waxy flesh, but their flavor is somewhat bland.

PENTLAND JAVELIN These new potatoes have very white, smooth skins and milky-white flesh. These potatoes are ideal for salads, but are also good boiled or steamed.

PENTLAND SQUIRE Usually white skinned, but occasionally russet, the flesh of these potatoes is very white. Their floury texture makes them perfect for baking. They are also good for boiling and mashing, but are poor in salads.

PINK FIR APPLE These knobby, misshapen potatoes have white skins with a pinkish blush and a pale-yellow flesh. They are firm and waxy, with a delicious nutty flavor, and have many of the characteristics of new potatoes. They are best cooked in their skins, as their shape makes them extremely difficult to peel, and are good steamed, boiled, and served cold in salads.

SHELAGH This Scottish variety has a creamy-colored flesh and pinkish patches all over the skin. The waxy texture of these potatoes makes them good for boiling, steaming, or frying.

SWEET POTATOES These potatoes are grown in tropical areas of the Americas and in many other hot countries around the world. Their skins are red, and the flesh inside is either white or orange. Orange-fleshed sweet potatoes have a denser, waxier texture and tend to hold their shape better, whereas white-fleshed ones are starchier and not quite as sugary. It is impossible to tell from the outside what color the flesh will be within, so, unless labeled, you may need to scrape off a small patch of skin. Treat in much the same way as ordinary potatoes—bake, mash, or fry.

YELLOW FINNS With a pale-yellow skin and flesh, these potatoes are suitable for all cooking methods and make particularly good french fries.

YUKON GOLD These potatoes have a yellow-colored flesh. They have a firm and dry texture and are great for baking, boiling, mashing, or frying. Yukon Gold potatoes are not so suitable for salads.

BUYING AND STORAGE

When buying potatoes, always choose ones with smooth, firm skins. When purchasing new potatoes, check that they are really young and fresh by scraping the skin—it should peel away very easily. Only buy the quantity you need and use within a couple of days. Check main crop potatoes to make sure that they are firm and not sprouting or showing any signs of mold. Avoid buying, and discard any potatoes with greenish patches or carefully cut them out. These parts of the potato are toxic and a sign that they have been stored in light.

Potatoes should be stored in a cool, dark place, but not in the refrigerator as the dampness will make them sweat, causing mold to grow. If the potatoes come in plastic bags, take them out and store in a paper bag or on a vegetable rack. If you prefer to buy in bulk, keep the potatoes in a cold, dark, dry place, such as a pantry or garage, making sure that they do not freeze in cold weather.

Sweet potatoes should be stored in a cool, dry place, but unlike ordinary potatoes, do not need to be kept in the dark.

VARIETIES OF RICE AND STORAGE

R ice is the staple food of many countries throughout the world. Every country and culture has its own repertoire of rice recipes; for example, India has the aromatic biryani, Spain has the saffron-scented paella, and Italy has the creamy risotto. Rice is grown on marshy, flooded land where other cereals cannot thrive and, because it is grown in so many different areas, there is a huge range of rice varieties.

LONG-GRAIN WHITE RICE This is probably the most widely used type of rice. Long-grain white rice has been milled so that

the husk, bran, and germ are removed. If you buy it loose, it is sometimes whitened with chalk or other substances, so thorough rinsing under cold running water is essential. Easy-cook, long-grain white rice has been steamed under pressure before milling. This makes it difficult to overcook, therefore separate dry and fluffy grains are virtually guaranteed. Precooked rice, also known as "parboiled" or "converted," is polished white rice that is half cooked after milling, then dried again. It is quick and simple to cook, but has a rather bland flavor. Java rice is one of the slightly shorter long-grain rices, and because it is particularly absorbent, it is often used in baked rice dishes.

Rice is sometimes referred to by the country or region in which it was originally grown. "Patna rice" is a term used to describe a type of long-grain rice which originated from Patna in northeast India. Long-grain rice is rarely labeled by country of origin, as it now mostly comes from America. "Carolina" is simply another name for long-grain rice and refers to the region in America where rice was first planted.

LONG-GRAIN BROWN RICE Here

the outer husk is removed, leaving the bran and germ behind, and so it retains a lot more of the fiber, vitamins, and minerals. It has a nutty, slightly chewy texture, and because it is less refined, it takes longer to cook than long-grain white rice.

BASMATI RICE This slender long-grain rice, which may be white or brown, is grown in the foothills of the Himalayas.

After harvesting, it is allowed to mature for a year, giving it a unique aromatic flavor, hence its name, which means "fragrant." Its perfect, separate, white, and fluffy grains frequently feature in Indian cooking.

RISOTTO RICE Grown in the north of Italy, this is the only rice that is suitable for making Italian risotto. The grains are plump and stubby, and have the ability to absorb large quantities of liquid without becoming too soft, cooking to a creamy texture with a slight bite. The starchiness of risotto rice makes it a good addition to soups where it acts as thickener. It can also be made into molded rice dishes, such as timbales, as the grains hold together without being too sticky. There are two grades of risotto rice: superfino and fino. Arborio rice is the most widely sold variety of the former, but you may also find carnaroli, Roma, and baldo in Italian food shops and delicatessens. Fino rice, such as vialone nano, has a slightly shorter grain, but the flavor is still excellent.

VALENCIA RICE Traditionally used for Spanish paella, Valencia rice is soft and tender when ready. The medium-sized grains break down easily, so should be left unstirred during cooking to absorb the flavor of the stock and other ingredients.

JASMINE RICE Also known as "Thai fragrant rice," this long-grain rice has a delicate, almost perfumed, aroma and flavor and has a soft, sticky texture.

GLUTINOUS RICE White or black (unpolished), these short grains are high in starch and feature in Chinese and Japanese cooking. This rice has a slightly sweet taste and is used for making dim sum, as well as sweet, sticky puddings. As the grains are very sticky, they are good to use when making rice balls or rice pockets in lotus leaves.

JAPANESE SUSHI RICE When cooked, this rice clings together but individual grains still remain. When

RICE PRODUCTS

Numerous Japanese ingredients are made from rice. Japan's national drink, sake, is a spirit distilled from rice and is often used in cooking. Mirin is a sweet rice wine used as a marinade in dishes like teriyaki. Rice vinegar is made from soured and fermented wine. Japanese rice vinegar has a soft, mellow flavor, whereas Chinese rice vinegar has a very sharp taste.

Sometimes Japanese rice vinegars are made into flavored vinegars by mixing the vinegar with soy sauce, for example, to make dashi. Most rice vinegars are a clear, pale golden color, but brown rice vinegar, made from whole-grain rice, is deep brown.

Amasake is a rice drink often sold in health-food stores and is made by adding enzymes to whole-grain pudding rice. It can be used in desserts as an alternative to milk.

Rice wrappers, often used for spring rolls, are made from a mixture of rice flour, salt, and water. Machines roll the mixture out until it is extremely thin and transparent, then it is dried out. These wrappers come in hard circles or triangles that are easily softened by placing between two dampened dishtowels. When soft, the wrappers can be wrapped around a filling, then steamed or fried.

mixed with rice vinegar it is easy to roll up with a filling inside to make sushi. Much of the sushi rice eaten in the West is now grown in California.

PUDDING RICE This rounded, short-grain rice is ideal for puddings and rice desserts. The grains swell and absorb large quantities of milk during cooking, giving puddings a rich and soft, creamy consistency. Brown pudding rice is also available.

RED RICE This is grown in small amounts in the Camargue, a marshy region in Provence, in France. It is similar to brown rice in taste and texture, but when cooked its red color develops, making it an attractive addition to salads and other rice dishes.

WILD RICE Strictly speaking, this is an aquatic grass, which is grown in North America, rather than a true variety of rice. It may only be harvested in the manner of Native American harvesters. The black grains are long and slender and, after harvesting and cleaning, they are toasted to remove the chaff and intensify the nutty flavor and slight chewiness. It is often sold as a mixture with either long-grain white or basmati rice.

FLAKED RICE White or brown rice grains are steamed and rolled to paper thinness to make flaked rice. It is extremely quick to cook and is mainly used to make creamy puddings, but may also be used for baking. It is sometimes found in commercially made muesli mixtures.

GROUND RICE This type of rice is made by grounding white rice to the size of fine sand. Like flaked rice, it can be used to make rice puddings and is also frequently used in baking, especially for making cookies such as shortbread.

RICE FLOUR Raw rice can be ground finely to make rice flour, which may be used to thicken sauces (you need about 1 tablespoon to thicken 1¼ cups of liquid) or as a vital ingredient in sticky Asian cakes and desserts. It is also used to make fresh and dried rice noodles. When rice flour is ground even more finely, it becomes rice powder and has a fine consistency like cornstarch. It can be found in Asian food stores.

BUYING AND STORING RICE

Rice will keep for several years if kept in sealed packets, however, it is at its best when fresh. To ensure freshness, always buy rice from reputable shops with a good turnover and buy in small quantities. Once opened, store the rice in an airtight container in a cool, dry place to keep out moisture. Most rices (but not risotto) benefit from washing before cooking—tip into a sieve and rinse under cold running water for a minute or so, until the water runs clear.

Cooked rice will keep well for up to two days if cooled rapidly and stored in a bowl covered with plastic wrap in the refrigerator. If eating rice cold, serve within 24 hours—after this time it should be reheated thoroughly. To reheat rice, place it in a heavy-based saucepan with 2–3 tablespoons of water, cover, and heat until piping hot, shaking the pan occasionally. Alternatively, reheat the bowl of cooled rice in the microwave, piercing the plastic wrap first.

COOKING TECHNIQUES FOR POTATOES

Generally, new potato varieties have a firm and waxy texture that do not break up during cooking, so are ideal for boiling, steaming, and salads. Main crop potatoes, on the other hand, have a more floury texture and lend themselves to mashing and roasting—both types are suitable for french fries. When cooking potatoes, it is important to make sure the potatoes that you are using are the correct type for the dish being prepared. Whichever way you choose to serve potatoes, allow 6–8 oz. per person.

BOILING POTATOES

NEW POTATOES

Most of the new potatoes available nowadays are fairly clean—especially those sold in supermarkets—and simply need a light scrub before cooking in their skins. If the potatoes are very dirty, use a small scrubbing brush or scourer to remove both the skins and dirt. Add them to a pan of cold, salted water and bring to a boil. Cover the pan with a lid and simmer for 12–15 minutes or until tender. Add a couple of sprigs of fresh herbs to the pan if you like—fresh mint is traditionally used to flavor potatoes. Drain the potatoes thoroughly and serve hot with a little melted butter, or for a change, a tablespoon of pesto. The skins of first early new potatoes will peel away easily, but second earlies should be served in their skins or peeled when cooked (hold the hot potatoes with a fork to make this easier). Very firm new potatoes can be added to boiling water, simmered for 8 minutes, and then left to stand in the hot water for a further 10 minutes until cooked through.

OLD POTATOES

Choose a main crop potato suitable for boiling, then thinly peel and cut into even-sized pieces. Add to a saucepan of cold, salted water and bring to a boil. Cover the pan with a lid and simmer for 20 minutes or until tender.

Alternatively, you can cook the potatoes in their skins and peel them after cooking. It is particularly important to cook floury potatoes gently or the outsides may start to fall apart before they are tender in the center. Drain the potatoes in a colander, then return them to the pan to dry out over a very low heat for 1–2 minutes. If you are planning to serve the potatoes mashed, roughly mash them and add a pat of butter and 2 tablespoons of milk per potato. Mash until smooth, either with a hand masher, hand grater, or a potato ricer. Season to taste with salt, freshly ground black pepper, and a little freshly grated nutmeg, if desired, then beat for a few seconds with a wooden spoon until fluffy. As an alternative to butter, use a good-quality olive oil, or crème fraîche. Finely chopped red and green chilies, crispy-cooked crumbled bacon, fresh herbs, or grated Parmesan cheese can also be stirred in for additional flavor.

STEAMING POTATOES

All potatoes are suitable for steaming. This method of cooking is ideal for floury potatoes, as they fall apart easily when boiled.

New and small potatoes can be steamed whole, but larger ones should be cut into even-sized pieces. Place the potatoes in a steamer, colander, or sieve over boiling water and cover. Steam for 10 minutes if the potatoes are very small; if they are cut into large chunks, cook for 20–25 minutes.

FRYING POTATOES

FRENCH FRIES

To make french fries, wash, peel, and cut the potatoes into ⅜-in. slices. Cut the slices into long strips about ⅜ in. wide. Place the strips in a bowl of cold water and leave for 20 minutes, then drain and dry well on paper towels—moisture will make the fat spit. Pour some oil into a deep, heavy-based saucepan or deep-fat fryer, making sure that the oil does not go any further than halfway up the sides of the pan. Heat the oil to 375° F, or until a french fry dropped into the fat rises to the surface right away and is surrounded by bubbles. Put the french fries into a wire basket, lower into the oil, and cook for 7–8 minutes or until golden. Remove and increase the heat of the oil to 400° F. Lower the fries into the oil again and cook for 2–3 minutes or until they are crisp and golden brown. Drain on paper towels before serving.

Slightly finer fries are known as pommes frites, even finer ones as pommes allumettes, and the finest of all as pommes pailles. Paper-thin slices of peeled potatoes cut with a sharp knife, or using a mandoline or food processor, can be deep-fried a few at a time to make chips.

To make lower-fat french fries, preheat the oven to 400° F and place a nonstick baking tray in the oven to heat up. Cut the potatoes into french fries or into chunky wedges, if preferred. Put the fries or wedges in a pan of cold water and quickly bring to a boil. Simmer for 2 minutes, then drain in a colander. Leave for a few minutes to dry, then drizzle over 1½–2 tablespoons of olive or sunflower oil, and toss to coat. Tip onto the heated baking tray and cook in the preheated oven for 20–25 minutes, turning occasionally until golden brown and crisp.

SAUTÉED POTATOES

Cut peeled potatoes into rounds about ¼ in. thick and pat dry. Heat 2 tablespoons butter and 2 tablespoons of oil in a large, heavy-based skillet until hot. Add the potatoes in a single layer and cook for 4–5 minutes until the undersides are golden. Turn with a large fish slice and cook the other side until golden and tender. Drain on paper towels, and sprinkle with a little salt before serving.

BAKING POTATOES

Allow a ⅔-¾ lb. potato per person and choose a variety such as Maris Piper, Cara, or King Edward. Wash and dry the potatoes, prick the skins lightly, then rub each one with a little oil and sprinkle with salt. Bake at 400° F for 1–1½ hours or until the skins are crisp and the centers are very soft. To speed up the cooking time, thread onto metal skewers as this conducts heat to the middle of the potatoes.

ROASTING POTATOES

For crisp and brown outsides and fluffy centers, choose potatoes suitable for baking. Thinly peel the potatoes and cut into even-sized pieces. Drop them into a pan of boiling, salted water and simmer for 5 minutes. Turn off the heat and leave for a further 3–4 minutes. Drain well and return the potatoes to the pan over a low heat for a minute to dry them and to roughen the edges. Carefully transfer them to a roasting pan containing hot oil. Baste well, then bake at 425° F for 20 minutes. Turn them and cook for an additional 20–30 minutes, turning and basting at least one more time. Serve as soon as the potatoes are ready.

POTATO CROQUETTES

Mash dry, boiled potatoes with just a little butter or olive oil, then stir in 1 egg yolk mixed with 1–2 tablespoons of milk or crème fraîche to make a firm mixture. Shape the mashed potatoes into small cylinders about 2 in. long, rolling them in flour. Dip in beaten egg and then in fresh, white breadcrumbs. Chill the croquettes in the refrigerator for 30 minutes. Place a little butter and oil in a heavy-based skillet, and slowly heat until the butter has melted. Shallow fry the croquettes, turning occasionally, until they are golden brown and crisp.

ROSTI

Parboil peeled, waxy potatoes in boiling, salted water for 8 minutes, drain, and leave to cool before coarsely grating into a bowl. Season well with salt, freshly ground black pepper, and freshly chopped herbs, if desired. Heat a mixture of butter and oil in a heavy-based skillet until bubbling. Add tablespoonfuls of the grated potato to the pan and flatten with the back of a fish slice. Cook over a medium heat for about 7 minutes or until crisp and golden. Turn and cook the other side.

COOKING POTATOES IN A CLAY POT

Terra-cotta pots can cook up to 1 lb. of whole potatoes at a time. Soak the clay pot for at least 20 minutes before use, then add even-sized, preferably smallish potatoes. Drizzle a little olive oil over the top, and season generously with salt and freshly ground black pepper. Cover the pot with the lid and put in a cold oven, setting the temperature to 400° F. The potatoes will take about 45 minutes to cook.

MICROWAVED POTATOES

This method of cooking is suitable for boiling and baking potatoes, providing you do not want the skins to be crispy. To cook new potatoes, prick the skins with a skewer to prevent them from bursting, then place in a bowl with 3 tablespoons of boiling water. Cover with plastic wrap which has been pierced two or three times, and cook on high for 12–15 minutes, or until tender. Peeled chunks of potato can be cooked in the same way. To bake potatoes, place each potato on a circle of paper towels. Make several cuts in each to ensure that the skins do not burst. Transfer to the microwave plate and cook on high for 4–6 minutes per potato, allowing an extra 3–4 minutes for every additional potato. Turn the potatoes at least once during cooking. Let stand for 5 minutes before serving.

HEALTH AND NUTRITION

Potatoes are high in complex carbohydrates, providing sustained energy. They are also an excellent source of vitamins B and C, and minerals such as iron and potassium. They contain almost no fat and are high in dietary fiber.

COOKING TECHNIQUES FOR RICE

There are countless ways to cook rice, and there are even more opinions about how to do so! Much of course depends on the variety and brand of rice being used, the dish being prepared, and the desired results. Each variety of rice has its own characteristics. Some types of rice cook to light, separate grains, some to a rich, creamy consistency, and some to a consistency where the grains stick together. It is important, therefore, to ensure that the appropriate rice is used. Different types of rice have very different powers of absorption. Long-grain rice will absorb about three times its weight in water, whereas just 2 tablespoons of plump and short-grained pudding rice can soak up a massive 1¼ cups of liquid.

COOKING LONG-GRAIN RICE

By far the simplest method of cooking long-grain rice—whether white, brown, or basmati—is to add it to plenty of boiling, salted water in a large saucepan, so that the rice grains can move freely and do not stick together. Allow about ⅓ cup of rice per person when cooking as an side dish. Rinse it under cold, running water until clear—this removes any starch still clinging to the grains—then put it into the rapidly boiling water. Stir once and then when the water comes back to a boil, turn down the heat a little and simmer uncovered, allowing 10–12 minutes for white rice and 30–40 minutes for brown (check the timings on the box, as brands of rice vary). The easiest way to test if the rice is cooked is to bite a couple of grains—they should be tender but still firm. Drain the rice right away, then return it to the pan with a little butter and herbs if desired. Fluff the grains with a fork and serve. If you need to keep the rice warm, put it in a bowl and place over a pan of barely simmering water. Cover the top of the bowl with a clean dishtowel until ready to serve.

ABSORPTION METHOD

Cooking rice using the absorption method is also very simple and is favored by many because no draining is involved, and therefore no water is wasted. Also, by using this method, stock and other flavorful ingredients can be added and will be absorbed by the rice. Furthermore,

valuable nutrients are retained that would otherwise be lost in the cooking water when drained. To cook rice this way, measure the quantity of rice you need, then rinse it in a sieve under cold running water and pour it into a large heavy-based saucepan. If desired, you can cook the rice in a little butter or oil for about 1 minute. Pour in two parts water to one part rice (or use stock if you prefer), season with salt, and bring to a boil uncovered. Cover the pan with a tight-fitting lid, then simmer gently without lifting the lid until the liquid is absorbed and the rice is tender. White rice will take 15 minutes to cook, whereas brown rice will take about 35 minutes. It is important to simmer over a very low heat or the liquid will cook away before the rice is ready. Do not be tempted to check the rice too often while it is cooking as you will let out steam and therefore moisture. If there is still a little liquid left when the rice is tender, remove the lid and cook for about a minute until evaporated. Remove

from the heat and let stand with the lid on for 4–5 minutes. Do not rinse the rice when it is cooked, just fluff up with a fork before serving. This method is also good for cooking Jasmine and Valencia rice.

OVEN-BAKED METHOD

The oven-baked method also works by absorption. It takes a little longer than cooking rice on the burner, but is ideal to add to the oven if you are roasting, or simmering a casserole.

To make oven-baked rice for two people, gently fry a chopped onion in 1 tablespoon of olive oil in a casserole dish until the onion is soft and golden (leave the onion out if preferred). Add ½ cup long-grain rice and cook for 1 minute, then stir in 1¼ cups of chicken or vegetable stock—you can also add a finely pared strip of lemon zest or a bay leaf at this stage for an extra bit of flavor. Cover the casserole with a lid or aluminum foil, and bake on the middle shelf of a preheated oven at 350° F for 40 minutes or until the rice is tender and all the stock has been absorbed. Fluff up with a fork and serve immediately.

COOKING IN THE MICROWAVE

Rinse long-grain white or brown rice in cold running water, then place in a large heatproof bowl. Add boiling water or stock to the bowl, allowing 1¼ cups for ¾ cup rice and 2¼ cups for 1⅓ cups rice. Add a pinch of salt and a pat of butter, if desired. Cover with plastic wrap, making a few air holes to allow the steam to escape, and microwave on high for 3 minutes. Stir, then re-cover, and microwave on medium for 12 minutes for white rice and 25 minutes for brown. Let stand, covered, for 5 minutes before fluffing up with a fork and serving.

IN A PRESSURE COOKER

Follow the quantities given for the absorption method and bring to a boil in the pressure cooker. Stir once, cover with the lid and bring to a high 15 lb. pressure. Lower the heat and cook for 5 minutes for white rice or 8 minutes for brown rice.

IN A RICE COOKER

Follow the quantities given for the absorption method. Put the rice, salt, and boiling water or stock in the cooker, bring back to a boil, and cover. When all the liquid has been absorbed the cooker will turn itself off automatically.

WILD RICE

This type of rice can be cooked by any of the methods used for long-grain rice, however the cooking time required is longer. It will take between 35–50 minutes to cook wild rice, depending on whether you like your rice slightly chewy or very tender. To speed up the cooking time by 5–10 minutes, soak the rice in cold water first for 30 minutes. This also increases the volume of the rice when it is cooked.

RED RICE

Cook this in the same way as brown rice, as this type of rice has a very hard grain. It is best to cook the rice for about 40–60 minutes if you like your rice really tender—it will still keep its shape.

RISOTTO RICE

Most rices should not be stirred during cooking as it breaks up the grains and makes them soggy. Risotto rice is different, as it can absorb nearly five times its weight in liquid and still retain its shape. A good risotto has a creamy texture with a slight bite to the individual grains and is made by adding the cooking liquid gradually and stirring almost continuously during cooking.

For a classic risotto (known as "alla Milanese") for four people, place 1 tablespoon of olive oil and a pat of butter in a large heavy-based saucepan. Slowly heat the butter and oil until the butter has melted. Add 1 chopped onion to the pan and cook until tender. Add ⅔ cup of dry white wine and boil rapidly until it is almost totally reduced. Stir in 1¾ cups risotto rice. Add 4¾ cups boiling vegetable or chicken stock a ladleful at a time—each ladleful should be completely absorbed by the rice before the next one is added. Continue adding the stock until the rice is tender. This will take about 15–20 minutes. (It may not be necessary to add all of the stock to achieve the desired consistency.) Serve the risotto right away, sprinkled with grated Parmesan cheese. The basic risotto can be flavored in many ways. Try adding a couple of bay leaves, a lemongrass stalk, or a large pinch of saffron to the stock. Alternatively, use more red or white wine and less stock.

GLUTINOUS RICE

This rice is steamed (instead of being cooked in boiling water), until the grains are soft, tender, and stick together in a mass. Cooking times vary slightly according to the brand, so check the instructions on the package for specific directions.

PUDDING RICE

For a simple rice pudding, put ⅓ cup of pudding rice in a buttered ovenproof dish with sugar to taste. Pour 2½ cups near-boiling milk over the mixture, and bake in a preheated oven at 300° F for 30 minutes. Stir, then bake for an additional 1–1¼ hours until tender. Vary the flavor by infusing the milk with orange zest, adding nuts and dried fruit to the mixture, or using 1¼ cups coconut milk or light cream, and 1¼ cups of milk, instead of milk alone.

HEALTH AND NUTRITION

Rice has been the dietary staple of the East for centuries, where it has provided a healthy, balanced diet and has added substance to the small quantities of meat used in Eastern cooking. It is low in fat and high in complex carbohydrates, which are absorbed slowly and so help to maintain blood sugar levels. Rice is also a reasonable source of protein and provides most of the B vitamins, and the minerals potassium and phosphorus. It is also a gluten-free cereal, making it suitable for celiacs. Like other unrefined grains, brown rice is richer in nutrients and fiber than refined white rice.

RUTABAGA, TURNIP, PARSNIP, & POTATO SOUP

INGREDIENTS   Serves 4

2 large onions, peeled
2 tbsp. butter
2 medium carrots, peeled and roughly chopped
1 cup peeled and roughly chopped rutabaga
¾ cup peeled and roughly chopped turnip
¾ cup peeled and roughly chopped parsnips

1 cup peeled and roughly chopped potatoes
4¼ cups vegetable stock
½ tsp. freshly grated nutmeg
salt and freshly ground black pepper
4 tbsp. vegetable oil, for frying
½ cup heavy cream
warm crusty bread, to serve

1 Finely chop 1 onion. Melt the butter in a large saucepan and add the onion, carrots, rutabaga, turnip, parsnip, and potatoes. Cover and cook gently for about 10 minutes, without browning, stirring occasionally.

2 Add the stock, and season to taste with the nutmeg, salt, and pepper. Cover and bring to a boil, then reduce the heat and simmer gently for 15–20 minutes or until the vegetables are tender. Remove from the heat and let cool for 30 minutes.

3 Heat the oil in a large heavy-based skillet. Add the onions and cook over a medium heat for about 2–3 minutes, stirring frequently, until golden brown. Remove the onions with a slotted spoon and drain well on paper towels. As they cool, they will turn crispy.

4 Pour the cooled soup into a food processor or blender, and process to form a smooth purée. Return to the cleaned pan, adjust the seasoning, then stir in the cream. Gently reheat, and top with the crispy onions. Serve immediately with chunks of bread.

HELPFUL HINT

For a lower-fat version of this delicious soup, add milk (skim milk if desired) rather than cream when reheating.

POTATO & FENNEL SOUP

INGREDIENTS   Serves 4

2 tbsp. butter
2 large onions, peeled and
   thinly sliced
2–3 garlic cloves, peeled and
   crushed
1 tsp. salt
2 medium potatoes, about
   1 lb. in weight, peeled and
   diced

1 fennel bulb, trimmed and
   finely chopped
½ tsp. caraway seeds
4¼ cups vegetable stock
freshly ground black pepper
2 tbsp. freshly chopped parsley
4 tbsp. crème fraîche
roughly torn pieces of French
   bread, to serve

1 Melt the butter in a large heavy-based saucepan. Add the onions with the garlic and half the salt, and cook over a medium heat, stirring occasionally for 7–10 minutes or until the onions are very soft and beginning to turn brown.

2 Add the potatoes, fennel bulb, caraway seeds, and the remaining salt. Cook for about 5 minutes, then pour in the vegetable stock. Bring to a boil, partially cover, and simmer for 15–20 minutes or until the potatoes are tender. Stir in the chopped parsley and adjust the seasoning to taste.

3 For a smooth-textured soup, allow to cool slightly, then pour into a food processor or blender and blend until smooth. Reheat the soup gently, then ladle into individual soup bowls. For a chunky soup, omit this blending stage and ladle straight from the saucepan into soup bowls.

4 Swirl a spoonful of crème fraîche into each bowl and serve immediately with roughly torn pieces of French bread.

FOOD FACT

A fennel bulb is, in fact, the swollen stem of a plant known as "Florence fennel." Originating in Italy, Florence fennel has a distinct aniseed flavor, which mellows and sweetens when cooked. Look for well-rounded bulbs with bright green fronds. Fennel is at its best when fresh, so use as soon as possible after buying. It may be stored in the refrigerator for a few days.

CAWL

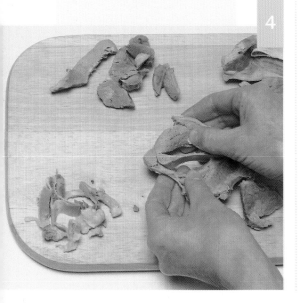

INGREDIENTS

Serves 4–6

1½ lbs. neck slices or rib chops of lamb
pinch of salt
2 large onions, peeled and thinly sliced
3 large potatoes, peeled and cut into chunks
2 parsnips, peeled and cut into chunks

1 rutabaga, peeled and cut into chunks
3 large carrots, peeled and cut into chunks
2 leeks, trimmed and sliced
freshly ground black pepper
4 tbsp. freshly chopped parsley
warm, crusty bread, to serve

1 Put the lamb in a large saucepan, cover with cold water, and bring to a boil. Add a generous pinch of salt. Simmer gently for 1½ hours, then set aside to cool completely, preferably overnight.

2 The next day, skim the fat off the surface of the lamb liquid and discard. Return the saucepan to the heat and bring back to a boil. Simmer for 5 minutes. Add the onions, potatoes, parsnips, rutabaga, and carrots, and return to a boil. Reduce the heat, cover, and cook for about 20 minutes, stirring occasionally.

3 Add the leeks and season to taste with salt and pepper. Cook for an additional 10 minutes or until all the vegetables are tender.

4 Using a slotted spoon, remove the meat from the saucepan, and take it off the bone. Discard the bones and any gristle, then return the meat to the pan. Adjust the seasoning to taste, stir in the parsley, then serve immediately with plenty of warm, crusty bread.

FOOD FACT

Many traditional Welsh recipes, such as cawl, feature lamb. This soup was once a staple dish, originally made with scraps of mutton or lamb and vegetables cooked together in a broth. Use Welsh lamb if possible for this modern version. The meat is lean and tender, and may have the delicate flavor of herbs if the sheep have been grazing on the wild thyme and rosemary that grow in the mountains.

POTATO, LEEK, & ROSEMARY SOUP

INGREDIENTS   Serves 4

¼ cup butter

1 lb. leeks, trimmed and finely sliced

4 cups peeled and roughly chopped potatoes

3¾ cups vegetable stock

4 sprigs of fresh rosemary

2 cups whole milk

2 tbsp. freshly chopped parsley

2 tbsp. crème fraîche

salt and freshly ground black pepper

whole-wheat rolls, to serve

1 Melt the butter in a large saucepan, add the leeks, and cook gently for 5 minutes, stirring frequently. Remove 1 tablespoon of the cooked leeks and set aside for garnishing.

2 Add the potatoes, vegetable stock, rosemary sprigs, and milk. Bring to a boil, then reduce the heat, cover, and simmer gently for 20–25 minutes or until the vegetables are tender.

3 Cool for 10 minutes. Discard the rosemary, then pour into a food processor or blender, and blend well to form a smooth-textured soup.

4 Return the soup to the cleaned saucepan and stir in the chopped parsley and crème fraîche. Season to taste with salt and pepper. If the soup is too thick, stir in a little more milk or water. Reheat gently, without boiling, then ladle into warm soup bowls. Garnish the soup with the set-aside leeks and serve immediately with whole-wheat rolls.

TASTY TIP

This rosemary-scented version of vichyssoise is equally delicious served cold. Allow the soup to cool before covering, then chill in the refrigerator for at least 2 hours. The soup will thicken as it chills, so you may need to thin it to the desired consistency with more milk or stock, and season before serving. It is important to use fresh rosemary rather than dried for this recipe. If unavailable, use 2 bay leaves, or add a bruised, fresh lemongrass stalk.

CREAM OF SPINACH SOUP

INGREDIENTS   Serves 6–8

1 large onion, peeled and
  chopped
5 large garlic cloves, peeled
  and chopped
2 medium potatoes, peeled
  and chopped
3¼ cups cold water
1 tsp. salt
1 lb. spinach, washed and
  large stems removed

¼ cup butter
3 tbsp. flour
3¼ cups milk
½ tsp. freshly grated nutmeg
freshly ground black pepper
6–8 tbsp. crème fraîche or
  sour cream
warm foccacia bread, to serve

1 Place the onion, garlic, and potatoes in a large saucepan and cover with the cold water. Add half the salt and bring to a boil. Cover and simmer for 15–20 minutes or until the potatoes are tender. Remove from the heat and add the spinach. Cover and set aside for 10 minutes.

2 Slowly melt the butter in another saucepan, add the flour, and cook over a low heat for about 2 minutes. Remove the saucepan from the heat and add the milk a little at a time, stirring continuously. Return to the heat and cook, stirring continuously for 5–8 minutes or until the sauce is smooth and slightly thickened. Add the freshly grated nutmeg or pepper to taste.

3 Blend the cooled potato and spinach mixture in a food processor or blender to a smooth purée, then return to the saucepan and gradually stir in the white

sauce. Season to taste with salt and pepper, and gently reheat, taking care not to allow the soup to boil. Ladle into soup bowls and top with spoonfuls of crème fraîche or sour cream. Serve immediately with warm foccacia bread.

HELPFUL HINT

When choosing spinach, always look for fresh, crisp, dark-green leaves. Store in a cool place until needed and use within 1–2 days of buying. To prepare, wash several times to remove any dirt or grit, and shake off as much excess water as possible or use a salad spinner. Remove the central stems only if they are large and tough—this is not necessary if you buy baby spinach leaves.

RICE & TOMATO SOUP

INGREDIENTS   Serves 4

heaping ¾ cup easy-cook
    basmati rice
1¾ cups chopped tomatoes
2 garlic cloves, peeled and
    crushed
grated zest of ½ lime
2 tbsp. extra-virgin olive oil
1 tsp. sugar
salt and freshly ground pepper

1¼ cups vegetable stock or
    water

FOR THE CROUTONS:
2 tbsp. prepared pesto sauce
2 tbsp. olive oil
6 thin slices ciabatta bread, cut
    into ½-in. cubes

1 Preheat the oven to 425° F.
Rinse and drain the basmati
rice. Place the tomatoes with
their juice in a large heavy-based
saucepan with the garlic, lime
zest, oil, and sugar. Season to
taste with salt and pepper. Bring
to a boil, then reduce the heat,
cover, and simmer for 10
minutes.

2 Add the boiling vegetable
stock or water and the rice,
then cook uncovered for an
additional 15–20 minutes or
until the rice is tender. If the
soup is too thick, add a little
more water. Set aside and keep
warm if the croutons are not
ready.

3 Meanwhile, to make the
croutons, mix the pesto and
olive oil in a large bowl. Add the
bread cubes and toss until they
are coated completely with the
mixture. Spread on a cookie
sheet, and bake in the preheated
oven for 10–15 minutes until

golden and crisp, turning them
over halfway through cooking.
Serve the soup immediately,
sprinkled with the warm croutons.

HELPFUL HINT

Pesto is a vivid green sauce
made from basil leaves and
olive oil. Store-bought pesto
is fine for this quick soup, but
try making your own during
the summer when fresh basil
is plentiful. To make ⅔ cup of
pesto, put 1 cup fresh basil
leaves, 1 peeled garlic clove,
1 tbsp. pine nuts, 4 tbsp. olive
oil, salt, and black pepper in a
blender or food processor
and blend together at high
speed until very creamy. Stir
in ¼ cup freshly grated
Parmesan cheese. Store in
the refrigerator for up to 2
weeks in an airtight jar.

COCONUT CHICKEN SOUP

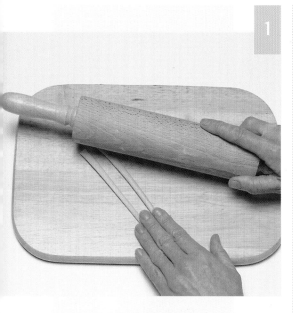

INGREDIENTS   Serves 4

2 lemongrass stalks
3 tbsp. vegetable oil
3 medium onions, peeled and finely sliced
3 garlic cloves, peeled and crushed
2 tbsp. fresh ginger, finely grated
2–3 kaffir lime leaves
1½ tsp. turmeric
1 red bell pepper, deseeded and diced
1¾ cups coconut milk

5 cups vegetable or chicken stock
1½ cups easy-cook long-grain rice
1½ cups roughly diced cooked chicken meat
1½ cups corn
3 tbsp. freshly chopped cilantro
1 tbsp. Thai fish sauce
freshly chopped pickled chilies, to serve

1 Discard the outer leaves of the lemongrass stalks, then place on a chopping board and, using a mallet or rolling pin, pound gently to bruise; set aside.

2 Heat the vegetable oil in a large saucepan and cook the onions over a medium heat for about 10–15 minutes until soft and beginning to change color.

3 Lower the heat, stir in the garlic, ginger, lime leaves, and turmeric, and cook for 1 minute. Add the red bell pepper, coconut milk, stock, lemongrass, and rice. Bring to a boil, cover, and simmer gently over a low heat for about 10 minutes.

4 Add the chicken and then stir it into the soup with the corn and the freshly chopped cilantro. Add a few dashes of

Thai fish sauce to taste, then reheat gently, stirring frequently. Serve immediately with a few chopped pickled chilies to sprinkle on top.

FOOD FACT

Small, dark, glossy kaffir lime leaves come from a wild citrus tree and are usually imported from southeast Asia. They impart a strong and sharp, spicy, citrus flavor and are frequently featured in Thai and Indonesian soups. If you have difficulty finding them, substitute a large strip of lime or lemon zest instead, remembering to remove before serving.

Hot & Sour Mushroom Soup

INGREDIENTS   Serves 4

4 tbsp. sunflower oil
3 garlic cloves, peeled and
   finely chopped
3 shallots, peeled and finely
   chopped
2 large red chilies, deseeded
   and finely chopped
1 tbsp. brown sugar
large pinch of salt
4¼ cups vegetable stock
1½ cups Thai fragrant rice
5 kaffir lime leaves, torn
2 tbsp. soy sauce

grated zest and juice of 1
   lemon
½ lb. oyster mushrooms,
   wiped and cut into pieces
2 tbsp. freshly chopped
   cilantro

TO GARNISH:
2 green chilies, deseeded and
   finely chopped
3 scallions, trimmed and finely
   chopped

1 Heat the oil in a skillet, add the garlic and shallots, and cook until golden brown and starting to crisp. Remove from the pan and set aside. Add the chilies to the pan and cook until they start to change color.

2 Place the garlic, shallots, and chilies in a food processor or blender. Blend to a smooth purée with ⅔ cup water. Pour the purée back into the pan, add the sugar with a large pinch of salt, then cook gently, stirring, until dark in color. Take care not to burn the mixture.

3 Pour the stock into a large saucepan, add the garlic purée, rice, lime leaves, soy sauce, and the lemon zest and juice. Bring to a boil, then reduce the heat, cover, and simmer gently for about 10 minutes.

4 Add the mushrooms and simmer for an additional 10 minutes or until the mushrooms and rice are tender. Remove the lime leaves, stir in the chopped cilantro, and ladle into bowls. Place the chopped green chilies and scallions in small bowls and serve separately to sprinkle on top of the soup.

HELPFUL HINT

There are many kinds of chilies, varying in both size and color, and many have a hot, spicy flavor. They contain volatile oils which can irritate your skin, so during preparation take great care not to touch your eyes, and wash your hands immediately after handling.

BACON & SPLIT PEA SOUP

INGREDIENTS   Serves 4

⅓ cup dried split peas
2 tbsp. butter
1 garlic clove, peeled and
   finely chopped
1 medium onion, peeled and
   thinly sliced
1 cup long-grain rice
2 tbsp. tomato paste
5 cups vegetable or chicken
   stock

1 cup peeled and finely diced
   carrots
4 slices bacon, finely chopped
salt and freshly ground black
   pepper
2 tbsp. freshly chopped
   parsley
4 tbsp. light cream
warm, crusty garlic bread, to
   serve

1 Cover the dried split peas with plenty of cold water, cover loosely, and leave to soak for a minimum of 12 hours, preferably overnight.

2 Melt the butter in a heavy-based saucepan, add the garlic and onion, and cook for 2–3 minutes, without browning. Add the rice, drained split peas, and tomato paste, and cook for 2–3 minutes, stirring constantly to prevent sticking. Add the stock, bring to a boil, then reduce the heat and simmer for 20–25 minutes or until the rice and peas are tender. Remove from the heat and let cool.

3 Blend about three quarters of the soup in a food processor, or blender, to form a smooth purée. Pour this into the remaining soup in the saucepan. Add the carrots and cook for an additional 10–12 minutes or until the carrots are tender.

4 Meanwhile, place the bacon in a nonstick skillet, and cook over a gentle heat until the bacon is crisp. Remove and drain on paper towels.

5 Season the soup with salt and pepper to taste, then stir in the parsley and cream. Reheat for 2–3 minutes, then ladle into soup bowls. Sprinkle with the bacon, and serve immediately with warm garlic bread.

HELPFUL HINT

You can use either green or yellow split peas for this satisfying soup—there is no difference in flavor. For a quicker alternative, use red split lentils, as they are quick to cook and do not need presoaking.

SQUASH & SMOKED HADDOCK SOUP

INGREDIENTS   Serves 4–6

2 tbsp. olive oil
1 medium onion, peeled and
   chopped
2 garlic cloves, peeled and
   chopped
3 celery stalks, trimmed and
   chopped
1½ lbs. squash, peeled,
   deseeded and cut into
   chunks

2⅔ cups peeled and coarsely
   diced potatoes
3¼ cups chicken stock, heated
½ cup dry sherry
½ lb. smoked haddock fillet
⅔ cup milk
freshly ground black pepper
2 tbsp. freshly chopped
   parsley

1 Heat the oil in a large heavy-based saucepan and gently cook the onion, garlic, and celery for about 10 minutes. This will release the sweetness but not brown the vegetables. Add the squash and potatoes to the saucepan and stir to coat the vegetables with the oil.

2 Gradually add the stock and bring to a boil. Cover, then reduce the heat and simmer for 25 minutes, stirring occasionally. Stir in the dry sherry, then remove the saucepan from the heat and let cool for 5–10 minutes.

3 Blend the mixture in a food processor, or blender, to form a chunky purée, and return to the cleaned saucepan.

4 Meanwhile, place the fish in a skillet. Pour in the milk with 3 tablespoons of water and bring almost to the boiling point. Reduce the heat, cover, and simmer for 6 minutes or until the fish is cooked and flakes easily. Remove from the heat and, using a slotted spoon, remove the fish from the liquid, setting aside both liquid and fish.

5 Discard the skin and any bones from the fish and flake into pieces. Stir the fish liquid into the soup, together with the flaked fish. Season with freshly ground black pepper, stir in the parsley, and serve immediately.

TASTY TIP

Use smoked salmon if haddock is unavailable. Butternut squash works nicely in this recipe.

Zucchini & Tarragon Tortilla

INGREDIENTS

Serves 6

1½ lbs. potatoes
3 tbsp. olive oil
1 onion, peeled and thinly
  sliced
salt and freshly ground black
  pepper

1 zucchini, trimmed and thinly
  sliced
6 medium eggs
2 tbsp. freshly chopped
  tarragon
tomato wedges, to serve

1 Peel the potatoes and slice thinly. Dry the slices in a clean dishtowel to get them as dry as possible. Heat the oil in a large heavy-based skillet, add the onion, and cook for 3 minutes. Add the potatoes along with a little salt and pepper, then stir the potatoes and onion lightly to coat in the oil.

2 Reduce the heat to the lowest possible setting, cover, and cook gently for 5 minutes. Turn the potatoes and onion over and continue to cook for an additional 5 minutes. Give the pan a shake every now and again to ensure that the potatoes do not stick to the base or burn. Add the zucchini, then cover and cook for 10 more minutes.

3 Beat the eggs and tarragon together, and season to taste with salt and pepper. Pour the egg mixture over the vegetables and return to the heat. Cook on a low heat for up to 20–25 minutes or until there is no liquid egg left on the surface of the tortilla.

4 Turn the tortilla over by inverting the pan onto the lid or a large flat plate. Slide the tortilla back into the pan. Return the pan to the heat and cook for a final 3–5 minutes or until the underside is golden brown. If preferred, place the tortilla under a preheated broiler for 4 minutes or until set and golden brown on top. Cut into small squares, and serve hot or cold with tomato wedges.

FOOD FACT

Almost regarded as the national dish of Spain, the tortilla is a substantial omelette traditionally made from eggs, potatoes, and onions. Here, zucchini and tarragon are added for extra flavor and color. Use even-sized, waxy potatoes, which do not break up during cooking.

SMOKED SALMON SUSHI

INGREDIENTS   Serves 4

¾ cup sushi rice or round long-
  grain pudding rice
2 tbsp. cider vinegar
1 tbsp. granulated sugar
1 tsp. salt
2 green leeks, trimmed

½ lb. smoked salmon
1 tsp. Japanese soy sauce

TO GARNISH:
fresh chives
lemon or lime wedges

1 Wash the rice in plenty of cold water, then drain. Put the rice and ¾ cup cold water in a saucepan, and leave to soak for 30 minutes. Place the saucepan over a medium heat and bring to a boil, stirring frequently. Lower the heat, cover, and cook the rice for about 15 minutes or until the grains are tender and the water has been absorbed. Remove from the heat and set aside, still covered, for an additional 10–15 minutes.

2 Place the vinegar, sugar, and salt in a small saucepan. Heat gently, stirring to dissolve the sugar. Turn the rice into a large bowl, sprinkle over the vinegar mixture, and mix together.

3 Cut the trimmed leeks in half lengthwise, then blanch in boiling water for 3–4 minutes. Drain, place in ice-cold water for 5 minutes, then drain again.

4 Separate the leek leaves. Cut both the leek leaves and the smoked salmon slices lengthwise into 1 x 3 in. strips, setting aside

2 wide leek leaves. Lay a leek slice neatly on top of each slice of smoked salmon.

5 Spoon the rice onto the salmon and leek slices, then roll. Using the tip of a sharp knife, slice the additional leek leaves lengthwise into long strips. Tie the strips around the smoked salmon rolls. Sprinkle the rolls with a few drops of the soy sauce, garnish with the chives and lemon wedges, and serve.

FOOD FACT

It takes many years of training to qualify as a sushi chef, but these smoked salmon and leek canapés are simple to make, although a little time consuming. Rolled sushi like these are known as *hosomaki* in Japan. Use the rice right after cooking—it cannot be stored in the refrigerator or it will harden and be difficult to work with.

POTATO PANCAKES

INGREDIENTS   Serves 6

FOR THE SAUCE:
4 tbsp. crème fraîche
1 tbsp. horseradish sauce
grated zest and juice of 1 lime
1 tbsp. freshly cut chives

1⅓ cups floury potatoes,
   peeled and coarsely diced
1 small egg white
2 tbsp. milk
2 tsp. self-rising flour

1 tbsp. freshly chopped thyme
large pinch of salt
a little vegetable oil, for frying
½ lb. smoked mackerel fillets,
   skinned and roughly
   chopped
fresh herbs, to garnish

1 To make the sauce, mix together the crème fraîche, horseradish, lime zest and juice, and chives. Cover and set aside.

2 Place the potatoes in a large saucepan, and cover with lightly salted, boiling water. Bring back to a boil, cover, and simmer for 15 minutes or until the potatoes are tender. Drain and mash until smooth. Cool for 5 minutes, then beat in the egg white, milk, flour, thyme, and salt to form a thick, smooth batter. Let stand for 30 minutes, then stir before using.

3 Heat a little oil in a heavy-based skillet. Add 2–3 large spoonfuls of batter to make a small pancake and cook for 1–2 minutes until golden. Turn the pancake over and cook for an additional minute or until golden. Repeat with the rest of the batter to make 8 pancakes.

4 Arrange the pancakes on a plate and top with the smoked mackerel. Garnish with herbs and serve immediately with spoonfuls of the horseradish sauce.

HELPFUL HINT

Keep the pancakes warm as you make them by stacking on a warmed plate. Place wax paper between each pancake to keep them separate, and fold a clean dishtowel loosely over the top. If desired, they can be made in advance and frozen, interleaved with nonstick baking parchment. To serve, thaw, then reheat the stack of pancakes, covered in aluminum foil, in a warm oven.

SWEET POTATO CHIPS WITH MANGO SALSA

INGREDIENTS   Serves 6

FOR THE SALSA:

1 large mango, peeled, pitted, and cut into small cubes

8 cherry tomatoes, quartered

½ cucumber, peeled and finely diced

1 red onion, peeled and finely chopped

pinch of sugar

1 red chili, deseeded and finely chopped

2 tbsp. rice vinegar

2 tbsp. olive oil

grated zest and juice of 1 lime

2⅔ cups peeled and thinly sliced sweet potatoes,

vegetable oil, for deep frying

sea salt

2 tbsp. freshly chopped mint

1 To make the salsa, mix the mango with the tomatoes, cucumber, and onion. Add the sugar, chili, vinegar, oil, and the lime zest and juice. Mix together thoroughly, cover, and leave for 45–50 minutes.

2 Soak the potatoes in cold water for 40 minutes to remove as much of the excess starch as possible. Drain and dry thoroughly on a clean dishtowel or paper towel.

3 Heat the oil to 375° F in a deep fryer. When at the correct temperature, place half the potatoes in the frying basket, then carefully lower the potatoes into the hot oil and cook for 4–5 minutes or until they are golden brown. Shake the basket often so that the potatoes do not stick together.

4 Drain the potato chips on paper towels, sprinkle with sea salt, and place under a preheated broiler for a few seconds to dry out. Repeat with the remaining potatoes. Stir the mint into the salsa and serve with the potato chips.

HELPFUL HINT

Take care when deep-fat frying. Use a deep heavy-based saucepan or special deep-fat fryer, and fill the pan by no more than one third with oil. If you do not have a food thermometer, check the temperature by dropping a cube of bread into the oil. At the correct heat, it will turn golden brown in 40 seconds.

STUFFED GRAPE LEAVES

INGREDIENTS   Serves 6–8

heaping ¾ cup long-grain rice
½ lb. fresh or preserved grape
  leaves
1 red onion, peeled and finely
  chopped
3 baby leeks, trimmed and
  finely sliced
1 cup freshly chopped parsley
1 cup freshly chopped mint
1 cup freshly chopped dill
⅔ cup extra-virgin olive oil
salt and freshly ground black
  pepper

¼ cup currants
½ cup finely chopped dried
  apricots
2½ tbsp. pine nuts
juice of 1 lemon
2½–3¼ cups boiling stock
lemon wedges or slices, to
  garnish
4 tbsp. plain yogurt, to serve

1 Soak the rice in cold water for 30 minutes. If using fresh vine leaves, blanch them, 5–6 leaves at a time, in salted, boiling water for a minute. Rinse and drain. If using preserved vine leaves, soak in tepid water for at least 20 minutes, drain, rinse, and pat dry with a paper towel.

2 Mix the onion and leeks with the herbs and half the oil. Add the drained rice, mix, and season with salt and pepper. Stir in the currants, apricots, pine nuts, and lemon juice. Spoon 1 teaspoon of the filling at the stalk end of each leaf. Roll, tucking the side flaps into the center to create a neat pocket. Continue until all the filling is used.

3 Layer half the remaining vine leaves over the base of a large

skillet. Put the little pockets in the skillet, and cover with the remaining leaves.

4 Pour in enough stock just to cover the vine leaves, add a pinch of salt, and bring to a boil. Reduce the heat, cover, and simmer for 45–55 minutes or until the rice is sticky and tender. Let stand for 10 minutes. Drain off any remaining stock. Garnish with lemon wedges, and serve hot with the yogurt.

FOOD FACT

The use of grape leaves in cooking goes back as far as the early cultivation of vines. Particularly popular in Middle Eastern cooking, they give a delicious, tart flavor to dishes.

POTATO SKINS

INGREDIENTS
Serves 4

4 large baking potatoes
2 tbsp. olive oil
2 tsp. paprika
¾ cup roughly chopped
   pancetta or bacon
6 tbsp. heavy cream
⅓ cup diced blue cheese, such
   as Gorgonzola

1 tbsp. freshly chopped
   parsley

TO SERVE:
mayonnaise
sweet chili dipping sauce
tossed green salad

1 Preheat the oven to 400° F. Scrub the potatoes, then prick a few times with a fork or skewer and place directly on the top shelf of the oven. Bake in the preheated oven for at least 1 hour or until tender. The potatoes are cooked when they yield gently to the pressure of your hand.

2 Set the potatoes aside until cool enough to handle, then cut in half and scoop the flesh into a bowl and set aside. Preheat the broiler, and line the pan with aluminum foil.

3 Mix together the oil and paprika, and use half to brush the outside of the potato skins. Place on the foil-lined pan under the preheated broiler, and cook for 5 minutes or until crisp, turning as necessary.

4 Heat the remaining paprika-flavored oil and gently fry the pancetta until crisp. Add to the potato flesh along with the cream, blue cheese, and parsley.

Halve the potato skins, and fill with the blue-cheese filling. Return to the oven for an additional 15 minutes to heat through. Sprinkle with a little more paprika, and serve immediately with mayonnaise, sweet chili sauce, and a green salad.

FOOD FACT

A popular Italian cheese, Gorgonzola was first made over 1100 years ago, in the village of the same name, near Milan. Now mostly produced in Lombardy, it is made from pasteurized cow's milk and allowed to ripen for at least 3 months, giving it a rich, but not overpowering, flavor. Unlike most blue cheeses, it should have a greater concentration of veining toward the center of the cheese.

RED BEET RISOTTO

INGREDIENTS   Serves 6

6 tbsp. extra-virgin olive oil
1 onion, peeled and finely
  chopped
2 garlic cloves, peeled and
  finely chopped
2 tsp. freshly chopped thyme
1 tsp. grated lemon zest
2 cups Arborio rice
⅔ cup dry white wine
3¾ cups vegetable stock,
  heated

2 tbsp. heavy cream
1½ cups peeled and finely
  chopped cooked beet
2 tbsp. freshly chopped
  parsley
¾ cup freshly grated Parmesan
  cheese
salt and freshly ground black
  pepper
sprigs of fresh thyme, to
  garnish

1 Heat half the oil in a large heavy-based skillet. Add the onion, garlic, thyme, and lemon zest. Cook for 5 minutes, stirring frequently, until the onion is soft and transparent, but not browned. Add the rice and stir until it is well coated in the oil.

2 Add the wine, then bring to a boil and boil rapidly until the wine has almost evaporated. Reduce the heat.

3 Keeping the pan over a low heat, add a ladleful of the hot stock to the rice, and cook, stirring constantly, until the stock is absorbed. Continue gradually adding the stock in this way until the rice is tender; this should take about 20 minutes. You may not need all the stock.

4 Stir in the cream, chopped beet, parsley, and half the grated Parmesan cheese. Season to taste with salt and pepper. Garnish with sprigs of fresh thyme, and serve immediately, with the remaining grated Parmesan cheese.

TASTY TIP

If you buy ready-cooked beets, choose small ones, which are sweeter. Make sure that they are not packed in vinegar (i.e., pickled), as this would spoil the flavor of the dish. If cooking your own, try baking them instead of boiling. Leave the stems intact and gently scrub to remove any dirt. Put them in a baking dish, cover loosely, and cook in a preheated oven at 325° F for 2 hours. Once cool enough to handle, the skins should slip right off.

GINGER & GARLIC POTATOES

INGREDIENTS

Serves 4

1½ lbs. potatoes
1-in. piece of ginger, peeled and coarsely chopped
3 garlic cloves, peeled and chopped
½ tsp. turmeric
1 tsp. salt
½ tsp. cayenne pepper
5 tbsp. vegetable oil
1 tsp. whole fennel seeds
1 large apple, cored and diced

6 scallions, trimmed and sliced diagonally
1 tbsp. freshly chopped cilantro

TO SERVE:
dark-green lettuce
mayonnaise, seasoned with curry to taste

1 Scrub the potatoes, then place, unpeeled, in a large saucepan and cover with boiling, salted water. Bring to a boil and cook for 15 minutes, then drain and leave the potatoes to cool completely. Peel and cut into 1-in. cubes.

2 Place the ginger, garlic, turmeric, salt, and cayenne pepper in a food processor and blend for 1 minute. With the motor still running, slowly add 3 tablespoons of water and blend into a paste. Alternatively, pound the ingredients to a paste with a mortar and pestle.

3 Heat the oil in a large heavy-based skillet and when hot, but not smoking, add the fennel seeds, and fry for a few minutes. Stir in the ginger paste, and cook for 2 minutes, stirring frequently. Take care not to burn the mixture.

4 Reduce the heat, then add the potatoes and cook for 5–7 minutes, stirring frequently, until the potatoes have a golden-brown crust. Add the diced apple and scallions, then sprinkle with the freshly chopped cilantro. Heat for 2 minutes, then serve on lettuce with curry-flavored mayonnaise.

FOOD FACT

Turmeric is a rhizome that comes from the same family as ginger. When the root is dried, it has a dull yellow appearance and can be ground to a powder. Turmeric powder can be used in a wide range of savory dishes. It has a warm, spicy flavor and gives food a wonderful golden color.

THAI CRAB CAKES

INGREDIENTS

Serves 4

heaping 1 cup easy-cook
   basmati rice
2 cups chicken stock, heated
½ lb. cooked crabmeat
¼ lb. white fish fillet, skinned
   and ground or finely
   chopped
5 scallions, trimmed and finely
   chopped
1 lemon grass stalk, outer
   leaves discarded and finely
   chopped
1 green chili, deseeded and
   finely chopped

1 tbsp. freshly grated ginger
1 tbsp. freshly chopped
   cilantro
1 tbsp. all-purpose flour
1 medium egg
salt and freshly ground black
   pepper
2 tbsp. vegetable oil, for frying

TO SERVE:
sweet chili dipping sauce
fresh lettuce

1 Put the rice in a large
saucepan and add the hot
stock. Bring to a boil, cover, and
simmer over a low heat, without
stirring, for 18 minutes or until
the grains are tender and all the
liquid is absorbed.

2 To make the cakes, place the
crabmeat, fish, scallions,
lemongrass, chili, ginger, cilantro,
flour, and egg in a food processor.
Blend until all the ingredients
are mixed thoroughly, then
season to taste with salt and
pepper. Add the rice to the
processor and blend once more,
but do not overmix.

3 Remove the mixture from the
processor, and place on a
clean work surface. With damp
hands, divide into 12 even-sized
patties. Transfer to a plate, cover,

and chill in the refrigerator for
about 30 minutes.

4 Heat the oil in a heavy-based
skillet and cook the crab cakes,
four at a time, for 3–5 minutes on
each side until crisp and golden.
Drain on paper towels and serve
immediately with a chili dipping
sauce.

HELPFUL HINT

For the best flavor and
texture, use freshly cooked
crab for this dish, choosing
the white rather than brown
meat. Canned crabmeat will
still give good results. Simply
drain in a sieve and rinse very
briefly under cold water to
remove the excess brine
before using.

RICE & PAPAYA SALAD

INGREDIENTS   Serves 4

1 cup easy-cook basmati rice
1 cinnamon stick, bruised
1 bird's eye chili, deseeded
  and finely chopped
zest and juice of 2 limes
zest and juice of 2 lemons
2 tbsp. Thai fish sauce
1 tbsp. light brown sugar
1 papaya, peeled and seeded
1 mango, peeled and stone
  removed

1 green chili, deseeded and
  finely chopped
2 tbsp. freshly chopped
  cilantro
1 tbsp. freshly chopped mint
1¼ cups finely shredded
  cooked chicken meat
½ cup chopped roasted
  peanuts
strips of pita bread, to serve

1 Rinse and drain the rice, and pour into a saucepan. Add 2 cups salted, boiling water and the cinnamon stick. Bring to a boil, reduce the heat to a very low setting, cover, and cook, without stirring, for 15–18 minutes or until all the liquid is absorbed. The rice should be light and fluffy, and have steam holes on the surface. Remove the cinnamon stick and stir in the zest from 1 lime.

2 To make the dressing, place the bird's eye chili, remaining zest and lime and lemon juice, fish sauce, and sugar in a food processor, and mix for a few minutes until blended. Alternatively, place all these ingredients in an airtight jar and shake vigorously until well blended. Pour half the dressing over the hot rice and toss until the grains glisten.

3 Slice the papaya and mango into thin slices, then place in a bowl. Add the chopped green chili, cilantro, and mint. Add the cooked chicken to the bowl with the chopped peanuts.

4 Add the remaining dressing to the chicken mixture and stir until all the ingredients are lightly coated. Spoon the rice onto a platter, pile the chicken mixture on top, and serve with strips of warm pita bread.

HELPFUL HINT

The papaya's skin turns from green, when unripe, to yellow and orange. To prepare, cut in half lengthwise, scoop out the black seeds with a spoon, and discard. Cut away the thin skin before slicing.

TRADITIONAL FISH PIE

INGREDIENTS   Serves 4

1 lb. white fish fillets, skinned
2 cups milk
1 small onion, peeled and
  quartered
salt and freshly ground black
  pepper
5 cups peeled and coarsely
  diced potatoes
¼ cup plus 3 tbsp. butter
¼ lb. large shrimp, peeled

2 large eggs, hard-boiled and
  quartered
7-oz. can corn, drained
2 tbsp. freshly chopped
  parsley
3 tbsp. all-purpose flour
½ cup shredded cheddar
  cheese

1 Preheat the oven to 400° F. Place the fish in a shallow skillet, pour 1¼ cups of the milk over, and add the onion. Season to taste with salt and pepper. Bring to a boil and simmer for 8–10 minutes until the fish is cooked. Remove the fish with a slotted spoon and place in a baking dish. Strain the cooking liquid and set aside.

2 Boil the potatoes until soft, then mash with the 3 tablespoons of butter and 2–3 tablespoons of the remaining milk. Set aside.

3 Arrange the shrimp and sliced eggs on top of the fish, then sprinkle with the corn and parsley.

4 Melt the remaining butter in a saucepan, stir in the flour, and cook gently for 1 minute, stirring. Whisk in the cooking liquid and remaining milk. Cook for 2 minutes or until thickened, then pour over the fish mixture and cool slightly.

5 Spread the mashed potato over the top of the pie and sprinkle the cheese over the top. Bake in the preheated oven for 30 minutes, until golden. Serve immediately.

TASTY TIP

Any variety of white fish may be used in this delicious dish. You could also used smoked fish, such as smoked cod or haddock, for a change. After simmering in milk, carefully remove any bones from the cooked fish. Serve with a selection of vegetables.

SEAFOOD RISOTTO

INGREDIENTS   Serves 4

¼ cup butter

2 shallots, peeled and finely chopped

1 garlic clove, peeled and crushed

2 cups Arborio rice

⅔ cup white wine

2½ cups fish or vegetable stock, heated

¾ cup whole cooked unpeeled large shrimp

10-oz. can baby clams

⅓ cup smoked salmon trimmings

2 tbsp. freshly chopped parsley

TO SERVE:

green salad

1 Melt the butter in a large, heavy-based saucepan, add the shallots and garlic, and cook for 2 minutes until slightly softened. Add the rice and cook for 1–2 minutes, stirring continuously, then pour in the wine and boil for 1 minute.

2 Pour in half the hot stock, bring to a boil, cover the saucepan, and simmer gently for 15 minutes, adding the remaining stock a little at a time. Continue to simmer for 5 minutes or until the rice is cooked and all the liquid is absorbed.

3 Meanwhile, prepare the seafood by peeling the shrimp, and removing their heads and tails. Drain the clams and discard the liquid. Cut the smoked salmon into thin strips.

4 When the rice has cooked, stir in the shrimp, clams, smoked salmon strips, and half the chopped parsley, then heat for 1–2 minutes until everything is piping hot. Turn into a serving dish, sprinkle with the remaining parsley and the Parmesan cheese, and serve immediately with a green salad.

TASTY TIP

A good-quality stock will make a huge difference to the finished flavor of this risotto. Rinse 2 lbs. fish bones and trimmings, and put in a large saucepan with 1 carrot, 1 onion, and 1 celery stalk, all peeled and roughly chopped, 1 bouquet garni, 4 peppercorns, and 3¾ cups cold water. Slowly bring to a boil, then skim. Cover and simmer for 30 minutes. Strain the stock through a fine sieve, cool, and chill in the refrigerator for up to 2 days. After chilling, boil vigorously before using.

SMOKED HADDOCK KEDGEREE

INGREDIENTS   Serves 4

1 lb. smoked haddock fillet
¼ cup butter
1 onion, peeled and finely
   chopped
2 tsp. mild curry powder
1 cup long-grain rice
2 cups fish or vegetable stock,
   heated
2 large eggs, hard-boiled and

peeled
2 tbsp. freshly chopped
   parsley
2 tbsp. whipping cream
   (optional)
salt and freshly ground black
   pepper
pinch of cayenne pepper

1 Place the haddock in a shallow skillet, and cover with 1¼ cups water. Simmer gently for 8–10 minutes or until the fish is cooked. Drain, then remove all the skin and bones from the fish, and flake into a dish. Keep warm.

2 Melt the butter in a saucepan and add the chopped onion and curry powder. Cook, stirring, for 3–4 minutes, or until the onion is soft, then stir in the rice. Cook for an additional minute, stirring continuously, then stir in the hot stock.

3 Cover and simmer gently for 15 minutes or until the rice has absorbed all the liquid. Cut the eggs into quarters or eighths, and add half to the mixture with half the parsley.

4 Carefully fold the cooked fish into the mixture and add the cream, if desired. Season to taste with salt and pepper. Heat the kedgeree until piping hot.

5 Transfer the mixture to a large dish, and garnish with the remaining quartered eggs and parsley, and season with a pinch of cayenne pepper. Serve immediately.

FOOD FACT

The word *khichri* means a "mixture," in Hindi. The British in India adapted this dish of lentils, rice and spices into kedgeree by adding smoked fish and hard-boiled eggs. If smoked haddock is unavailable, use smoked salmon instead.

Tuna-Fish Patties

INGREDIENTS Makes 8

2⅔ cups peeled and coarsely
   diced potatoes
¼ cup butter
2 tbsp. milk
14-oz. can tuna in oil
1 scallion, trimmed and finely
   chopped
1 tbsp. freshly chopped parsley
salt and freshly ground black
   pepper
2 medium eggs, beaten

2 tbsp. seasoned all-purpose
   flour
2 cups fresh white bread
   crumbs
4 tbsp. vegetable oil
4 hamburger buns

TO SERVE:
french fries
mixed salad
tomato chutney

1 Place the potatoes in a large
saucepan, cover with boiling
water, and simmer until soft.
Drain, then mash with 3
tablespoons of the butter and the
milk. Turn into a large bowl.
Drain the tuna, discarding the
oil, and flake into the bowl of
potatoes. Stir well to mix.

2 Add the scallion and parsley,
and season to taste with salt
and pepper. Add 1 tablespoon of
the beaten egg to bind the
mixture together. Chill in the
refrigerator for at least 1 hour.

3 Shape the chilled mixture
with your hands into 4 large
patties. First, coat the patties with
seasoned flour, then brush them
with the remaining beaten egg,
allowing any excess to drip back
into the bowl. Finally, coat them
evenly in the bread crumbs,
pressing the crumbs on with your
hands, if necessary.

4 Heat a little of the oil in a
skillet, and fry the patties for
2–3 minutes on each side, until
golden, adding more oil if
necessary. Drain on paper towels
and serve hot on buns with
french fries, mixed salad, and
chutney.

HELPFUL HINT

Drain the potatoes
thoroughly, and dry them
over a very low heat before
mashing with the milk and
butter to ensure the mixture
is not too soft to shape. If
time allows, cover the patties
with plastic wrap and chill in
the refrigerator for 30
minutes so that they are
really firm before cooking.

SALMON PATTIES

INGREDIENTS   Serves 4

1 lb. salmon fillet, skinned
salt and freshly ground black
  pepper
2⅔ cups peeled and coarsely
  diced potatoes
¼ cup butter
1 tbsp. milk
2 medium tomatoes, skinned,
  deseeded, and chopped
2 tbsp. freshly chopped parsley
1½ cups whole-wheat bread

crumbs
¼ cup shredded cheddar
  cheese
2 tbsp. all-purpose flour
2 medium eggs, beaten
3–4 tbsp. vegetable oil

TO SERVE:
raita
sprigs of fresh mint

1 Place the salmon in a shallow skillet, and cover with water. Season to taste with salt and pepper, and simmer for 8–10 minutes, until the fish is cooked. Drain and flake into a bowl.

2 Boil the potatoes in lightly salted water until soft, then drain. Mash with the butter and milk until smooth. Add the potato to the bowl of fish, and stir in the tomatoes and half the parsley. Adjust the seasoning to taste. Chill the mixture in the refrigerator for at least 2 hours to firm up.

3 Mix the bread crumbs with the cheese and the remaining parsley. When the fish mixture is firm, form into 8 patties. First, lightly coat the patties in the flour, then dip into the beaten egg, allowing any excess to drip back into the bowl. Finally, press the patties into the

bread-crumb mixture until well coated.

4 Heat a little of the oil in a skillet, and fry the patties in batches for 2–3 minutes on each side until golden and crisp, adding more oil if necessary. Serve with raita, garnished with sprigs of mint.

HELPFUL HINT

To remove the skins from the tomatoes, pierce each with the tip of a sharp knife, then plunge into boiling water and leave for up to 1 minute. After a cold-water rinsing, the skins should peel off easily.
Raita is a refreshing Indian condiment made of yogurt and flavored with mint.

Battered Fish & Chunky Fries

INGREDIENTS   Serves 4

1 package yeast
1¼ cups beer
2 cups all-purpose flour
1 tsp. salt
1½ lbs. potatoes
2 cups peanut oil
4 pieces thick white fish fillet,
    about ½ lb. each, skinned and
    boned

2 tbsp. seasoned all-purpose
    flour

TO GARNISH:
lemon wedges
sprigs of Italian parsley

1 Dissolve the yeast in a little of the beer in a pitcher, and mix to a paste. Pour in the remaining beer, whisking all the time until smooth. Place the flour and salt in a bowl, and gradually pour in the beer mixture, whisking continuously to make a thick, smooth batter. Cover the bowl and allow the batter to stand at room temperature for 1 hour.

2 Peel the potatoes and cut into thick slices. Cut each slice lengthwise to make chunky fries. Place them in a nonstick frying pan and heat, shaking the pan until all the moisture has evaporated. Turn them onto paper towels to dry off.

3 Heat the oil to 350° F, then fry the potatoes, a few at a time, for 4–5 minutes until crisp and golden. Drain on paper towels and keep warm.

4 Pat the fish fillets dry, then coat in the flour. Dip the floured fillets into the batter. Fry for 2–3 minutes until cooked and crisp, then drain. Garnish with lemon wedges and parsley, and serve immediately with the fries.

HELPFUL HINT

Yeast is a living, microscopic organism that converts food into alcohol and carbohydrates. When mixed with warm liquid, yeast produces gases which lighten this batter. Check that the yeast is moist and creamy-colored, and has a strong yeasty smell. If it is dry, discolored, and crumbly, it is probably stale and will not work well. Active dry yeast can be used instead. Follow the manufacturer's instructions for dry yeast.

PAELLA

INGREDIENTS   Serves 6

1 lb. live mussels

4 tbsp. olive oil

6 medium chicken thighs

1 medium onion, peeled and finely chopped

1 garlic clove, peeled and crushed

¾ cup skinned, deseeded and chopped tomatoes

1 red bell pepper, deseeded and chopped

1 green bell pepper, deseeded and chopped

⅔ cup frozen peas

1 tsp. paprika

2⅔ cups Arborio rice

½ tsp. turmeric

3¾ cups chicken stock, warmed

1 cup large shrimp, peeled

salt and freshly ground black pepper

2 limes

1 lemon

1 tbsp. freshly chopped basil

whole, cooked, unpeeled shrimp, to garnish

1 Rinse the mussels under cold running water, scrubbing well to remove any grit and barnacles, then pull off the hairy "beards." Tap any open mussels sharply with a knife, and discard if they refuse to close.

2 Heat the oil in a paella pan or large, heavy-based skillet, and cook the chicken thighs for 10–15 minutes until golden. Remove and keep warm.

3 Fry the onion and garlic in the remaining oil in the pan for 2–3 minutes, then add the tomatoes, peppers, peas, and paprika, and cook for an additional 3 minutes.

4 Add the rice to the pan and return the chicken with the turmeric and half the stock.

Bring to a boil and simmer, gradually adding more stock as it is absorbed. Cook for 20 minutes, or until most of the stock has been absorbed and the rice is almost tender.

5 Put the mussels in a large saucepan with 2 in. salted, boiling water, cover, and steam for 5 minutes. Discard any with shells that have not opened, then stir into the rice with the shrimp. Season to taste with salt and pepper. Heat for 2–3 minutes until piping hot. Squeeze the juice from 1 of the limes over the paella.

6 Cut the remaining limes and the lemon into wedges, and arrange on top of the paella. Sprinkle with the basil, garnish with the shrimp, and serve.

RUSSIAN FISH PIE

INGREDIENTS   Serves 4–6

1 lb. white fish fillet
⅔ cup dry white wine
salt and freshly ground black
 pepper
⅓ cup butter or margarine
1 large onion, peeled and
 finely chopped
½ cup long-grain rice
1 tbsp. freshly chopped dill
¼ lb. baby button mushrooms,
 quartered

¾ cup peeled, whole, cooked
 shrimp, thawed if frozen
3 medium eggs, hard-boiled
 and chopped
1¼ lbs. ready-made puff
 pastry, thawed if frozen
1 small egg, beaten with a
 pinch of salt
assorted lettuce, to serve

1 Preheat the oven to 400° F. Place the fish in a shallow skillet with the wine, ⅔ cup water, and salt and pepper. Simmer for 8–10 minutes. Strain the fish, setting aside the liquid, and, when cool enough to handle, flake into a bowl.

2 Melt the butter or margarine in a saucepan, and cook the onions for 2–3 minutes, then add the rice, remaining fish liquid, and dill. Season lightly. Cover and simmer for 10 minutes, then stir in the mushrooms and cook for an additional 10 minutes or until all the liquid is absorbed. Mix the rice with the cooked fish, shrimps, and eggs. Let cool.

3 Roll half the pastry out on a lightly floured surface into a 9 x 12 in. rectangle. Place on a dampened cookie sheet and arrange the fish mixture on top,

leaving a ½-in. border. Brush the border with a little water.

4 Roll out the remaining pastry to a rectangle and use to cover the fish. Brush the edges lightly with a little of the beaten egg and press to seal. Roll out the pastry trimmings and use to decorate the top. Chill in the refrigerator for 30 minutes. Brush with the beaten egg and bake for 30 minutes or until golden. Serve immediately with lettuce.

FOOD FACT

Kulebyaka, or koulubiac, is a classic festive dish from Russia. It is traditionally made with a yeast dough, but puff pastry works well as an easy alternative.

TUNA & MUSHROOM RAGOUT

INGREDIENTS

Serves 4

1⅓ cups mixed basmati and
  wild rice
¼ cup butter
1 tbsp. olive oil
1 large onion, peeled and
  finely chopped
1 garlic clove, peeled and
  crushed
¾ lb. baby button mushrooms,
  halved
2 tbsp. all-purpose flour
14-oz. can chopped tomatoes
1 tbsp. freshly chopped

parsley
dash of Worcestershire sauce
14 oz. canned tuna in oil,
  drained
salt and freshly ground black
  pepper
4 tbsp. grated Parmesan
  cheese
1 tbsp. freshly shredded basil

TO SERVE:
green salad
garlic bread

1 Cook the basmati and wild rice in a saucepan of boiling salted water for 20 minutes, then drain and return to the pan. Stir in half of the butter, cover the pan, and let stand for 2 minutes until the butter has melted.

2 Heat the oil and the remaining butter in a skillet, and cook the onion for 1–2 minutes until soft. Add the garlic and mushrooms, and continue to cook for an additional 3 minutes.

3 Stir in the flour and cook for 1 minute, then add the tomatoes and bring the sauce to a boil. Add the parsley, Worcestershire sauce, and tuna, and simmer gently for 3 minutes. Season to taste with salt and freshly ground pepper.

4 Stir the rice well, then spoon onto four serving plates, and top with the tuna and mushroom mixture. Sprinkle with a spoonful of grated Parmesan cheese and some shredded basil, and serve immediately with a green salad and chunks of garlic bread.

TASTY TIP

Fresh basil adds a wonderful flavor and fragrance to this dish, but sometimes it can be difficult to find during the winter months. If you have problems finding it, buy canned tomatoes that have basil already added to them, or use extra freshly chopped parsley instead.

COCONUT FISH CURRY

INGREDIENTS   Serves 4

2 tbsp. sunflower oil

1 medium onion, peeled and
very finely chopped

1 yellow bell pepper, deseeded
and finely chopped

1 garlic clove, peeled and
crushed

1 tbsp. mild curry paste

1-in. piece of ginger, peeled
and grated

1 red chili, deseeded and
finely chopped

14-oz. can coconut milk

1½ lb. firm white fish, skinned
and cut into chunks

1⅓ cups basmati rice

1 tbsp. freshly chopped
cilantro

1 tbsp. mango chutney

salt and freshly ground black
pepper

TO GARNISH:

lime wedges

fresh cilantro sprigs

TO SERVE:

plain yogurt

warm naan bread

1 Put 1 tablespoon of the oil into a large skillet and cook the onion, pepper, and garlic for 5 minutes or until soft. Add the remaining oil, curry paste, ginger, and chili, and cook for an additional minute.

2 Pour in the coconut milk and bring to a boil. Reduce the heat and simmer gently for 5 minutes, stirring occasionally. Add the fish to the pan and continue to simmer gently for 5–10 minutes or until the fish is tender, but not overcooked.

3 Meanwhile, cook the rice in a saucepan of salted boiling water for 15 minutes or until tender. Drain the rice thoroughly and turn out into a serving dish.

4 Stir the chopped cilantro and chutney gently into the fish curry, and season to taste with salt and pepper. Spoon the fish curry over the cooked rice, garnish with lime wedges and cilantro sprigs, and serve immediately with spoonfuls of plain yogurt and warm naan bread.

FOOD FACT

Coconut milk is the liquid extracted from grated and pressed coconut flesh, combined with a little water.

CHUNKY FISH CASSEROLE

INGREDIENTS Serves 6

¼ cup butter or margarine
2 large onions, peeled and
sliced into rings
1 red bell pepper, deseeded
and roughly chopped
1 lb. potatoes, peeled
1 lb. zucchini, trimmed and
thickly sliced
2 tbsp. all-purpose flour
1 tbsp. paprika
2 tsp. vegetable oil

1¼ cups white wine
⅔ cup fish stock
14-oz. can chopped tomatoes
2 tbsp. freshly chopped basil
salt and freshly ground black
pepper
1 lb. firm white fish fillet,
skinned and cut into 1-in.
cubes
sprigs of fresh basil, to garnish
freshly cooked rice, to serve

1 Melt the butter or margarine in a large saucepan, add the onions and pepper, and cook for 5 minutes or until softened.

2 Cut the peeled potatoes into 1-in. cubes, rinse lightly, and shake dry, then add them to the onions and pepper in the saucepan. Add the zucchini and cook, stirring frequently, for an additional 2–3 minutes.

3 Sprinkle the flour, paprika, and vegetable oil into the saucepan and cook, stirring continuously, for 1 minute. Pour in ⅔ cup of the wine, with all the stock, and the chopped tomatoes, and bring to a boil.

4 Add the basil to the casserole, season to taste with salt and pepper, and cover. Simmer for 15 minutes, then add the fish and the remaining wine, and simmer very gently for an additional 5–7

minutes, or until the fish and vegetables are just tender. Garnish with basil sprigs and serve immediately with freshly cooked rice.

FOOD FACT

Halibut has firm, milky white flesh that has an almost meaty texture, making it ideal for this casserole. They can grow to an enormous size, at times weighing in at over 450 lbs., and are fished in the deep, freezing-cold waters of the North Sea.

MEDITERRANEAN CHOWDER

INGREDIENTS

Serves 6

1 tbsp. olive oil

1 tbsp. butter

1 large onion, peeled and finely sliced

4 celery stalks, trimmed and thinly sliced

2 garlic cloves, peeled and crushed

1 bird's eye chili, deseeded and finely chopped

1 tbsp. all-purpose flour

1⅓ cups peeled and diced potatoes

2½ cups fish or vegetable stock

1½ lbs. white fish fillet, cut into 1-in. cubes

2 tbsp. freshly chopped parsley

¾ cup large peeled cooked shrimp

7-oz. can corn, drained

salt and freshly ground black pepper

⅔ cup light cream

1 tbsp. freshly cut chives

warm, crusty bread, to serve

1 Heat the oil and butter together in a large saucepan. Add the onion, celery, and garlic, and cook gently for 2–3 minutes until softened. Add the chili and stir in the flour. Cook, stirring, for an additional minute.

2 Add the potatoes to the saucepan with the stock. Bring to a boil, cover, and simmer for 10 minutes. Add the fish cubes to the saucepan with the chopped parsley, and cook for an additional 5–10 minutes or until the fish and potatoes are just tender.

3 Stir in the peeled shrimp and corn, and season to taste with salt and pepper. Pour in the cream and adjust the seasoning, if necessary.

4 Sprinkle the chives over the chowder. Ladle into six large bowls and serve immediately, with plenty of warm, crusty bread.

FOOD FACT

A chowder is a classic meal-in-a-bowl soup whose name originates from the French *chaudière* (the pot used by settlers in the southern states for making soups and stews). Chowders are usually fish based and often feature corn. This version has been thickened with potatoes.

SPANISH OMELETTE WITH SMOKED FISH

INGREDIENTS   Serves 3–4

3 tbsp. sunflower oil

2 cups peeled and diced
potatoes

2 medium onions, peeled and
cut into wedges

2–4 large garlic cloves, peeled
and thinly sliced

1 large red bell pepper,
deseeded, quartered, and
thinly sliced

¼ lb. smoked haddock

salt and freshly ground black
pepper

2 tbsp. butter, melted

1 tbsp. heavy cream

6 medium eggs, beaten

2 tbsp. freshly chopped Italian
parsley

½ cup shredded cheddar
cheese

TO SERVE:

crusty bread

tossed green salad, to serve

1 Heat the oil in a large,
nonstick, heavy-based skillet,
add the potatoes, onions, and
garlic, and cook gently for 10–15
minutes until golden brown, then
add the red bell pepper and cook
for 3 minutes.

2 Meanwhile, place the fish in
a shallow skillet and cover
with water. Season to taste with
salt and pepper, and poach gently
for 10 minutes. Drain and flake
the fish into a bowl, toss in the
melted butter and cream, adjust
the seasoning, and set aside.

3 When the vegetables are
cooked, drain off any excess
oil, and stir in the beaten egg
with the chopped parsley. Pour
the fish mixture over the top and

cook gently for 5 minutes or
until the eggs become firm.

4 Sprinkle with the cheese and
place the pan under a
preheated broiler. Cook for 2–3
minutes until the cheese is golden
and bubbling. Carefully slide the
omelette onto a large plate, and
serve immediately with plenty of
bread and salad.

HELPFUL HINT

For best results, Spanish
omelettes should be cooked
slowly until set. Finishing the
dish under the broiler gives it
a delicious golden look.

SUPREME BAKED POTATOES

INGREDIENTS   Serves 4

4 large baking potatoes
3 tbsp. butter
1 tbsp. sunflower oil
1 carrot, peeled and chopped
2 celery stalks, trimmed and
   finely chopped
7-oz. can white crabmeat

2 scallions, trimmed and finely
   chopped
salt and freshly ground black
   pepper
½ cup shredded cheddar
   cheese
tomato salad, to serve

1 Preheat the oven to 400° F. Scrub the potatoes and prick all over with a fork or insert long metal skewers. Place the potatoes in the preheated oven for 1–1½ hours, or until soft to the touch. Allow to cool a little, then cut in half.

2 Scoop out the cooked potato flesh and turn into a bowl, leaving a reasonably firm potato shell. Mash the cooked potato flesh, then mix in the butter, and mash until the butter has melted.

3 While the potatoes are cooking, heat the oil in a frying pan, and cook the carrot and celery for 2 minutes. Cover the pan tightly and continue to cook for another 5 minute or until the vegetables are tender.

4 Add the cooked vegetables to the bowl of mashed potatoes and mix well. Fold in the crabmeat and the scallions, then season to taste with salt and pepper.

5 Pile the mixture back into the potato shells and press in firmly. Sprinkle the cheese over the top and return the potato halves to the oven for 12–15 minutes until hot, golden, and bubbling. Serve immediately with a tomato salad.

TASTY TIP

Inserting metal skewers helps potatoes to cook more evenly and quickly, as heat is transferred via the metal to the centers of the potatoes during cooking. To give the skins a crunchier finish, rub them with a little oil and lightly sprinkle with salt before baking.

SMOKED SALMON QUICHE

INGREDIENTS   Serves 6

2 cups all-purpose flour
¼ cup butter
¼ cup shortening or lard
2 tsp. sunflower oil
1⅓ cup peeled and diced
  potato
1 cup shredded Gruyère
  cheese
½ cup smoked salmon
  trimmings
5 medium eggs, beaten

1¼ cups light cream
salt and freshly ground black
  pepper
1 tbsp. freshly chopped Italian
  parsley

TO SERVE:
mixed salad
baby new potatoes

1 Preheat the oven to 400° F. Blend the flour, butter, and shortening together until the mixture resembles fine bread crumbs. Blend again, adding sufficient water to make a firm, but pliable, dough. Use the dough to line a 9-in. quiche dish or pan, then chill in the refrigerator for 30 minutes. Bake blind with baking beans for 10 minutes.

2 Heat the oil in a small skillet, add the diced potatoes, and cook for 3–4 minutes until lightly browned. Reduce the heat and cook for 2–3 minutes or until tender. Let cool.

3 Sprinkle the cheese evenly over the base of the pastry case, then arrange the cooled potatoes on top. Add the smoked salmon in an even layer.

4 Beat the eggs with the cream, and season to taste with salt and pepper. Whisk in the parsley and pour the mixture carefully into the dish.

5 Reduce the oven to 350° F and bake for about 30–40 minutes or until the filling is set and golden. Serve hot or cold with a mixed salad and baby new potatoes.

TASTY TIP

Using lard or vegetable shortening with the butter makes a delicious crust, but you can use all butter if you prefer a richer flavor and color. Do not be tempted to leave out the chilling time for the pastry case. This allows the pastry to rest and helps to minimize shrinkage during baking.

SMOKED MACKEREL & POTATO SALAD

INGREDIENTS

Serves 4

½ tsp. dry mustard powder
1 large egg yolk
salt and freshly ground black
  pepper
⅔ cup sunflower oil
1–2 tbsp. lemon juice
1 lb. baby new potatoes
¼ cup butter
¾ lb. smoked mackerel fillets
  (or salmon if preferred)

4 celery stalks, trimmed and
  finely chopped
3 tbsp. creamed horseradish
⅔ cup crème fraîche
1 romaine lettuce, rinsed and
  roughly torn
8 cherry tomatoes, halved

1 Place the mustard powder and egg yolk in a small bowl with salt and pepper, and whisk until blended. Add the oil, drop by drop, into the egg mixture, whisking continuously. When the mayonnaise is thick, add the lemon juice, drop by drop, until a smooth, glossy consistency is formed. Set aside.

2 Cook the potatoes in salted, boiling water until tender, then drain. Cool slightly, then cut into halves or quarters, depending on size. Return to the saucepan and toss in the butter.

3 Remove and discard the skin from the mackerel fillets and flake into pieces. Add to the potatoes in the saucepan, together with the celery.

4 Blend 4 tablespoons of the mayonnaise with the horseradish and crème fraîche. Season to taste with salt and pepper, then add to the potato and mackerel mixture, and stir lightly.

5 Arrange the lettuce and tomatoes on four serving plates. Pile the smoked mackerel mixture on top of the lettuce, grind over a little pepper, and serve with the remaining mayonnaise.

HELPFUL HINT

When making mayonnaise, ensure that the ingredients are at room temperature, or it may curdle. For speed, it can be made in a food processor: briefly blend the mustard, yolk, seasoning, and lemon juice, then, with the motor running, slowly add the oil.

SEAFOOD RICE RING

INGREDIENTS   Serves 4

2 cups long-grain rice
½ tsp. turmeric
5 tbsp. sunflower oil
2 tbsp. white wine vinegar
1 tsp. Dijon mustard
1 tsp. granulated sugar
1 tbsp. mild curry paste
4 shallots, peeled and finely
  chopped
salt and freshly ground black
  pepper

¾ cup peeled, cooked shrimp,
  thawed if frozen
2 tbsp. freshly chopped
  cilantro
8 fresh large tiger shrimp, with
  shells on
4 sprigs of cilantro, to garnish
lemon wedges, to serve

1 Lightly oil a 5-cup ring mold, or line the mold with plastic wrap. Cook the rice in salted, boiling water with the turmeric for 15 minutes or until tender. Drain thoroughly. Whisk 4 tablespoons of the oil with the vinegar, mustard, and sugar to form a dressing, and pour over the warm rice. Set aside.

2 Heat the remaining oil in a saucepan, add the curry paste and shallots, and cook for 5 minutes or until the shallots are just softened. Fold into the dressed rice, season to taste with salt and pepper, and mix well. Let cool completely.

3 Stir in the shrimp and the chopped cilantro, and turn into the prepared ring mold. Press the mixture down firmly with a spoon, then chill in the refrigerator for at least 1 hour.

4 Invert the ring onto a serving plate, and fill the center with the tiger shrimp. Garnish with sprigs of cilantro. Serve immediately with lemon wedges.

HELPFUL HINT

Make sure that you use ordinary long-grain rice for this seafood ring—easy-cook varieties are pretreated so that the grains remain separate and do not stick together (the opposite of what you require here). A mixture of basmati and wild rice can be used, if desired.

CHEESY VEGETABLE & SHRIMP BAKE

INGREDIENTS   Serves 4

1 cup long-grain rice

salt and freshly ground black pepper

1 garlic clove, peeled and crushed

1 large egg, beaten

3 tbsp. freshly shredded basil

4 tbsp. grated Parmesan cheese

¼ lb. baby asparagus spears, trimmed

1 cup trimmed baby carrots

1 cup trimmed fine green beans

¼ lb. cherry tomatoes

1 cup peeled cooked shrimp, thawed if frozen

¼ lb. mozzarella cheese, thinly sliced

1 Preheat the oven to 400° F. Cook the rice in lightly salted, boiling water for 12–15 minutes or until tender and drain. Stir in the garlic, beaten egg, shredded basil, 2 tablespoons of the Parmesan cheese, and season to taste with salt, and pepper. Press this mixture into a greased 9-in. square, ovenproof dish and set aside.

2 Bring a large saucepan of water to a boil, then drop in the asparagus, carrots, and green beans. Return to a boil and cook for 3–4 minutes. Drain and let cool.

3 Quarter or halve the cherry tomatoes, and mix them into the cooled vegetables. Spread the prepared vegetables over the rice, and top with the shrimp. Season to taste with salt and pepper.

4 Cover the shrimp with the mozzarella, and sprinkle with the remaining Parmesan cheese. Bake in the preheated oven for 20–25 minutes until piping hot and golden brown in places. Serve immediately.

FOOD FACT

Mozzarella is a fresh-tasting unripened cheese, now produced throughout the world. Traditional mozzarella is made from buffalo milk, but cow's milk is commonly used or sometimes a mixture of the two. The cheese becomes stringy when cooked, so it should be sliced as thinly as possible here.

FISH CRUMBLE

INGREDIENTS

Serves 6

1 lb. white fish fillets
1¼ cups milk
salt and freshly ground black
   pepper
1 tbsp. sunflower oil
⅓ cup butter or margarine
1 medium onion, peeled and
   finely chopped
2 leeks, trimmed and sliced
1 medium carrot, peeled and
   diced
2 medium potatoes, peeled
   and cut into small pieces
1½ cups all-purpose flour

1½ cups fish or vegetable stock
2 tbsp. whipping cream
1 tsp. freshly chopped dill

FOR THE CRUMBLE TOPPING:
⅓ cup butter or margarine
1½ cups all-purpose flour
¾ cup grated Parmesan cheese
¾ tsp. cayenne pepper

1 Preheat the oven to 400° F. Grease a pie pan. Place the fish in a saucepan with the milk, salt, and pepper. Bring to a boil, cover, and simmer for 8–10 minutes until the fish is cooked. Remove with a slotted spoon, setting aside the cooking liquid. Flake the fish into the prepared dish.

2 Heat the oil and 1 tablespoon of the butter or margarine in a small skillet and gently fry the onion, leeks, carrot, and potatoes for 1–2 minutes. Cover tightly, and cook over a gentle heat for an additional 10 minutes until softened. Spoon the vegetables over the fish.

3 Melt the remaining butter or margarine in a saucepan, add the flour, and cook for 1 minute,

stirring. Whisk in the cooking liquid and the stock. Cook until thickened, then stir in the cream. Remove from the heat and stir in the dill. Pour over the fish.

4 To make the crumble, rub the butter or margarine into the flour until the mixture resembles bread crumbs, then stir in the cheese and cayenne pepper. Sprinkle over the dish, and bake in the oven for 20 minutes.

TASTY TIP

Vary the taste and texture of the topping by making it with whole-wheat flour, or by adding ¼ cup chopped nuts or jumbo rolled oats.

POTATO BOULANGÈRE WITH GROUPER

INGREDIENTS   Serves 2

2½ cups peeled and thinly
   sliced potatoes
1 large onion, peeled and
   thinly sliced
salt and freshly ground black
   pepper

1¼ cups fish or vegetable stock
⅓ cup butter or margarine
¾ lb. grouper or other white
   fish fillets
sprigs of fresh Italian parsley,
   to garnish

1 Preheat the oven to 400° F. Lightly grease a shallow baking dish with oil or butter. Layer the potato slices and onions alternately in the prepared dish, seasoning each layer with salt and pepper.

2 Pour the stock over the top, then cut ¼ cup of the butter or margarine into small pieces and dot over the top layer. Bake in the preheated oven for 50–60 minutes. Do not cover the dish at this stage.

3 Lightly rinse the fish fillets and pat dry on paper towels. Cook on a griddle, or heat the remaining butter or margarine in a skillet and pan-fry the fish fillets for 3–4 minutes per side, flesh side first. Remove from the pan with a fish slice and drain on paper towels.

4 Remove the partly cooked potato and onion mixture from the oven and place the fish on the top. Cover with

aluminum foil and return to the oven for 10 minutes until heated through. Garnish with sprigs of parsley and serve immediately.

FOOD FACT

The grouper family of fish includes several Atlantic and Pacific varieties. These fish generally have firm, white flesh with a mild, slightly sweet flavor. Any other white fish can be used in this dish, if desired. Serve this dish with a selection of freshly cooked green vegetables.

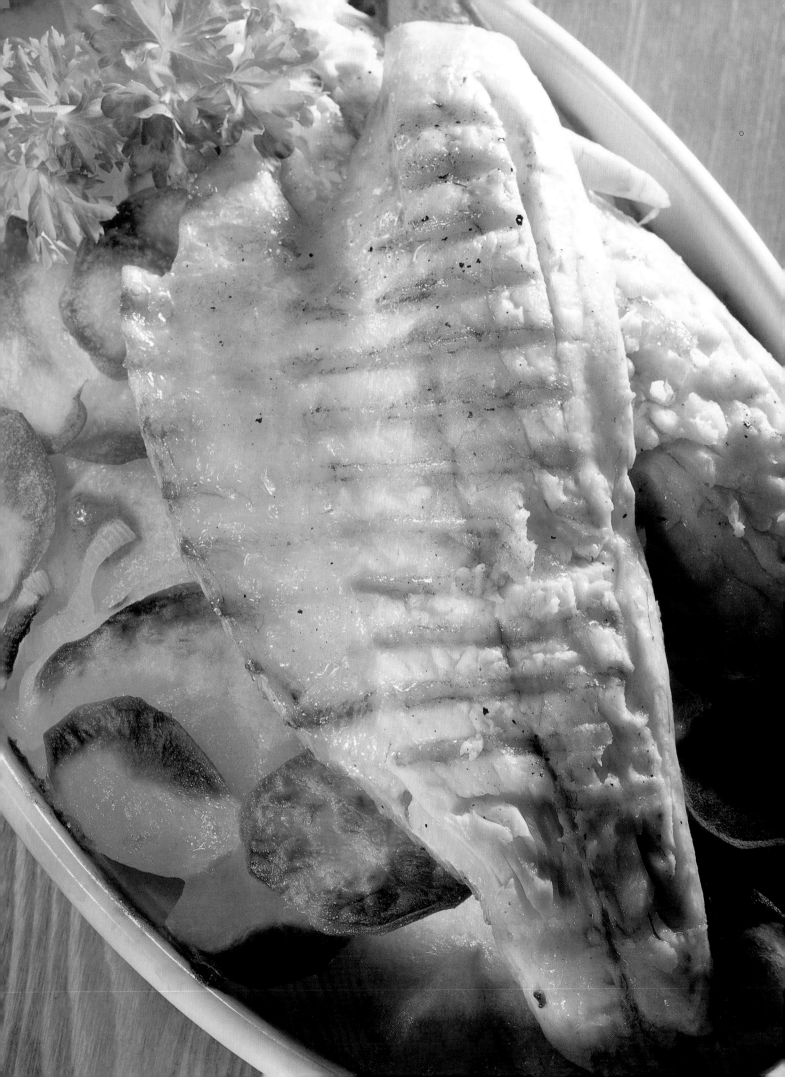

JAMAICAN JERK PORK WITH RICE & PEAS

INGREDIENTS
Serves 4

2 onions, peeled and chopped
2 garlic cloves, peeled and crushed
4 tbsp. lime juice
2 tbsp. each dark molasses, soy sauce, and chopped fresh ginger
2 jalapeño chilies, deseeded and chopped
½ tsp. ground cinnamon
¼ tsp. each ground allspice and ground nutmeg
4 pork loin chops, on the bone
1 cup dried red kidney beans, soaked overnight

FOR THE RICE:
1 tbsp. vegetable oil
1 onion, peeled and finely chopped
1 celery stalk, trimmed and finely sliced
3 garlic cloves, peeled and crushed
2 bay leaves
1⅓ cups long-grain white rice
2¼ cups chicken or ham stock
sprigs of fresh Italian parsley, to garnish

1 To make the jerk pork marinade, purée the onions, garlic, lime juice, molasses, soy sauce, ginger, chilies, cinnamon, allspice, and nutmeg together in a food processor until smooth. Put the pork chops into a plastic or nonreactive dish, and pour over the marinade, turning the chops to coat. Marinate in the refrigerator for at least 1 hour or overnight.

2 Drain the beans and place in a large saucepan with about 9 cups cold water. Bring to a boil and boil rapidly for 10 minutes. Reduce the heat, cover, and simmer gently for 1 hour until tender, adding more water if necessary. When cooked, drain well and mash roughly.

3 Heat the oil for the rice in a saucepan with a tight-fitting lid, and add the onion, celery, and garlic. Cook gently for 5 minutes until softened. Add the bay leaves, rice, and stock, and stir. Bring to a boil, cover, and cook very gently for 10 minutes. Add the beans and stir well again. Cook for an additional 5 minutes, then remove from the heat.

4 Heat a griddle until almost smoking. Remove the pork chops from the marinade, scraping off any surplus and place on the griddle. Cook for 5–8 minutes on each side, or until cooked. Garnish with parsley and serve immediately with the rice.

PORK LOIN STUFFED WITH ORANGE & HAZELNUT RICE

INGREDIENTS   Serves 4

1 tbsp. butter
1 shallot, peeled and finely
  chopped
⅓ cup long-grain brown rice
¾ cup vegetable stock
½ orange
⅓ cup pitted and chopped
  prunes
¼ cup roasted and roughly
  chopped hazelnuts
1 small egg, beaten

1 tbsp. freshly chopped
  parsley
salt and freshly ground pepper
1 lb. boneless pork tenderloin
  or fillet, trimmed

FOR THE RICE:
steamed zucchini
carrots

1 Preheat the oven to 375° F. Heat the butter in a small saucepan, add the shallot, and cook gently for 2–3 minutes until softened. Add the rice and stir well for 1 minute. Add the stock, stir well, and bring to a boil. Cover tightly and simmer gently for 30 minutes, until the rice is tender and all the liquid is absorbed. Let cool.

2 Grate the orange zest and set aside. Remove the white pith and chop the orange flesh finely. Mix together the orange zest and flesh, prunes, hazelnuts, cooled rice, egg, and parsley. Season to taste with salt and pepper.

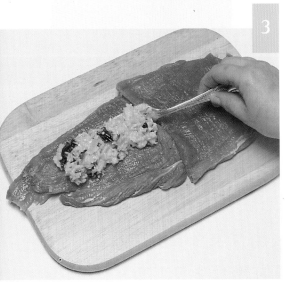

3 Cut the pork in half, then, using a sharp knife, split the meat lengthwise almost in two, forming a pocket, leaving it just attached. Open out the pork and put between 2 pieces of plastic wrap. Flatten using a meat mallet until about half its original thickness. Spoon the filling into the pocket and close the fillet over. Tie along the length with kitchen string at regular intervals.

4 Put the pork fillet in a small roasting pan and cook in the top of the preheated oven for 25–30 minutes, or until the meat is just tender. Remove from the oven and allow to rest for 5 minutes. Slice into rounds and serve with steamed zucchini and carrots.

TASTY TIP

For an alternative stuffing, try adding pine nuts and thyme.

PORK GOULASH & RICE

INGREDIENTS

Serves 4

1½ lbs. boneless pork rib chops

1 tbsp. olive oil

2 onions, peeled and roughly chopped

1 red bell pepper, deseeded and thinly sliced

1 garlic clove, peeled and crushed

1 tbsp. all-purpose flour

1 rounded tbsp. paprika

14-oz. can chopped tomatoes

salt and freshly ground black pepper

1½ cups long-grain white rice

2 cups chicken stock

sprigs of fresh Italian parsley, to garnish

⅔ cup sour cream, to serve

1 Preheat the oven to 275° F. Cut the pork into large cubes, about 1½ in. square. Heat the oil in a large flameproof casserole and brown the pork in batches over a high heat, transferring the cubes to a plate as they brown.

2 Over a medium heat, add the onions and pepper, and cook for about 5 minutes, stirring regularly, until they begin to brown. Add the garlic, and return the meat to the casserole along with any juices on the plate. Sprinkle in the flour and paprika, and stir well to soak up the oil and juices.

3 Add the tomatoes and season to taste with salt and pepper. Bring slowly to a boil, cover with a tight-fitting lid, and cook in the preheated oven for 1½ hours.

4 Meanwhile, rinse the rice in several changes of water until the water remains relatively clear.

Drain well and put into a saucepan with the chicken stock or water and a little salt. Cover tightly and bring to a boil. Turn the heat down as low as possible and cook for 10 minutes, without removing the lid. After 10 minutes, remove from the heat, and leave for an additional 10 minutes, without removing the lid. Fluff with a fork.

5 When the meat is tender, lightly stir in the sour cream to create a marbled effect, or serve separately. Garnish with parsley, and serve with the rice.

FOOD FACT

Paprika is the ground red dried pepper, *Capsicum annum*; it is a vital ingredient of goulash, giving it a distinctive color and flavor.

LAMB PILAF

INGREDIENTS
Serves 4

2 tbsp. vegetable oil
¼ cup flaked or slivered
  almonds
1 medium onion, peeled and
  finely chopped
1 medium carrot, peeled and
  finely chopped
1 celery stalk, trimmed and
  finely chopped
¾ lb. lean lamb, cut into
  chunks
¼ tsp. ground cinnamon
¼ tsp. chili flakes
2 large tomatoes, skinned,
  deseeded, and chopped

grated zest of 1 orange
2 cups easy-cook brown
  basmati rice
2½ cups vegetable or lamb
  stock
2 tbsp. freshly cut chives
3 tbsp. freshly chopped
  cilantro
salt and freshly ground black
  pepper

TO GARNISH:
lemon slices
sprigs of cilantro

1 Preheat the oven to 275° F. Heat the oil in a flameproof casserole dish with a tight-fitting lid, and add the almonds. Cook, stirring often, for about 1 minute, until just browning. Add the onion, carrot, and celery, and cook gently for an additional 8–10 minutes until soft and lightly browned.

2 Increase the heat and add the lamb. Cook for an additional 5 minutes until the lamb has changed color. Add the ground cinnamon and chili flakes. Stir briefly before adding the tomatoes and orange zest.

3 Stir and add the rice, then the stock. Bring slowly to a boil and cover tightly. Transfer to the preheated oven and cook for 30–35 minutes until the rice is tender and the stock is absorbed.

4 Remove from the oven and leave for 5 minutes before stirring in the chives and cilantro. Season to taste with salt and pepper. Garnish with the lemon slices and sprigs of cilantro, and serve immediately.

TASTY TIP

The lamb in this aromatic pilaf is cooked for a relatively short time, so choose a tender cut such as leg, shoulder, or fillet. If you buy the meat on the bone, use the bones to make a stock—it will make all the difference to the final flavor of the dish.

Nasi Goreng

INGREDIENTS Serves 4

7 large shallots, peeled
1 red chili, deseeded and
 roughly chopped
2 garlic cloves, peeled and
 roughly chopped
4 tbsp. sunflower oil
2 tsp. each tomato paste and
 Indonesian sweet soy sauce
 (*katjap manis*)
1⅓ cups long-grain white rice
¾ cup trimmed green beans
3 medium eggs, beaten
pinch of sugar

salt and freshly ground black
 pepper
2½ cups shredded cooked ham
1½ cups peeled, cooked
 shrimp, thawed if frozen
6 scallions, trimmed and thinly
 sliced
1 tbsp. light soy sauce
3 tbsp. freshly chopped
 cilantro

1 Roughly chop one of the shallots and place with the red chili, garlic, 1 tablespoon of the oil, tomato paste, and sweet soy sauce in a food processor, and blend until smooth, then set aside. Boil the rice in plenty of salted water for 6–7 minutes until tender, adding the French beans after 4 minutes. Drain well and allow to cool.

2 Beat the eggs with the sugar and a little salt and pepper. Heat a little of the oil in a small nonstick skillet and add about one third of the egg mixture. Swirl to coat the base of the pan thinly, and cook for about 1 minute until golden. Flip and cook the other side briefly before removing from the pan. Roll the omelette, and slice thinly into strips. Repeat with the remaining egg to make 3 omelettes.

3 Thinly slice the remaining shallots, then heat an additional 2 tablespoons of the oil in a clean skillet. Cook the shallots for 8–10 minutes over a medium heat until golden and crisp. Drain on paper towels and set aside.

4 Add the remaining 1 tablespoon of oil to a large wok or skillet, and fry the chili paste over a medium heat for 1 minute. Add the cooked rice and beans, and stir-fry for 2 minutes. Add the ham and shrimp, and continue stir-frying for an additional 1–2 minutes. Add the omelette slices, half the fried shallots, the scallions, soy sauce, and chopped cilantro. Stir-fry for an additional minute until heated through. Spoon onto serving plates and garnish with the remaining crispy shallots. Serve immediately.

Leek & Ham Risotto

INGREDIENTS Serves 4

1 tbsp. olive oil
2 tbsp. butter
1 medium onion, peeled and finely chopped
4 leeks, trimmed and thinly sliced
1½ tbsp. freshly chopped thyme
2 cups Arborio rice

5½ cups vegetable or chicken stock, heated
½ lb. cooked ham
1¼ cups peas, thawed if frozen
½ cup grated Parmesan cheese
salt and freshly ground black pepper

1 Heat the oil and half the butter together in a large saucepan. Add the onion and leeks, and cook over a medium heat for 6–8 minutes, stirring occasionally, until soft and beginning to color. Stir in the thyme and cook briefly.

2 Add the rice and stir well. Continue stirring over a medium heat for about 1 minute until the rice is glossy. Add a ladleful or two of the stock, and stir well until the stock is absorbed. Continue adding stock, a ladleful at a time, stirring well between additions, until about two thirds of the stock has been added.

3 Meanwhile, either chop or finely shred the ham, then add to the saucepan of rice, together with the peas. Continue adding ladlefuls of stock, as described in step 2, until the rice is tender and the ham is heated through completely.

4 Add the remaining butter, sprinkle with the Parmesan cheese, and season to taste with salt and pepper. When the butter has melted and the cheese has softened, stir well to incorporate. Taste and adjust the seasoning, then serve immediately.

HELPFUL HINT

Risotto should take about 15 minutes to cook, so taste it after this time—the rice should be creamy, with just a slight bite to it. If it is not quite ready, continue adding the stock, a little at a time, and cook for a few more minutes. Stop as soon as it tastes ready, as you do not have to add all of the liquid.

ROAST LEG OF LAMB & BOULANGÈRE POTATOES

INGREDIENTS   Serves 6

2½ lbs. potatoes, peeled
1 large onion, peeled and
    finely sliced
salt and freshly ground black
    pepper
2 tbsp. olive oil
¼ cup butter
¼ cup lamb stock

½ cup milk
4½ lb. leg of lamb
2–3 sprigs of fresh rosemary
6 large garlic cloves, peeled
    and finely sliced
6 anchovy fillets, drained
extra sprigs of fresh rosemary,
    to garnish

1 Preheat the oven to 450° F. Finely slice the potatoes—a mandolin is the best tool for this. Layer the potatoes with the onion in a large roasting pan, seasoning each layer with salt and pepper. Drizzle about 1 tablespoon of the olive oil over the potatoes, and add the butter in small pieces. Pour in the lamb stock and milk. Set aside.

2 Make small incisions all over the lamb with the point of a small, sharp knife. Into each incision, insert a small piece of rosemary, a sliver of garlic, and a piece of anchovy fillet.

3 Drizzle the rest of the olive oil over the leg of lamb and its flavorings, and season well. Place the meat directly onto a shelf in the preheated oven. Position the roasting pan of potatoes directly underneath to catch the juices during cooking. Roast for 15 minutes per pound—about 1 hour for a leg of this size—reducing the oven temperature to 400° F after 20 minutes.

4 When the lamb is cooked, remove from the oven and allow to rest for 10 minutes before carving. Meanwhile, increase the temperature to 450°F, and cook the potatoes for an additional 10–15 minutes to become crisp. Garnish and serve.

FOOD FACT

Leg of lamb is one of the prime roasting joints and may weigh between 4–6 lbs., so when you visit the butcher, ask for a small joint. This dish is delicious served with a selection of winter vegetables, such as freshly cooked broccoli and carrots.

LANCASHIRE HOTPOT

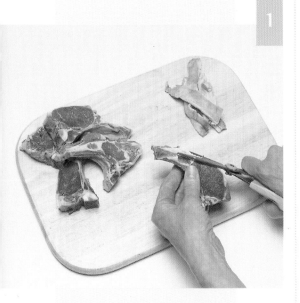

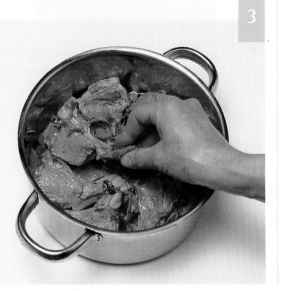

INGREDIENTS
Serves 4

2¼ lbs. neck slices or rib chops of lamb

2 tbsp. vegetable oil

2 large onions, peeled and sliced

2 tsp. all-purpose flour

⅔ cup vegetable or lamb stock

3¾ cups peeled and thickly sliced waxy potatoes

salt and freshly ground black pepper

1 bay leaf

2 sprigs of fresh thyme

1 tbsp. melted butter

2 tbsp. freshly chopped herbs, to garnish

freshly cooked green beans, to serve

1 Preheat the oven to 325° F. Trim any excess fat from the lamb. Heat the oil in a skillet, and brown the pieces of lamb in batches for 3–4 minutes each. Remove with a slotted spoon and set aside. Add the onions to the pan and cook for 6–8 minutes until softened and just beginning to brown, then set aside.

2 Stir in the flour and cook for a few seconds, then gradually pour in the stock, stirring well, and bring to a boil. Remove from the heat.

3 Spread the bottom of a large casserole dish with half the potato slices. Top with half the onions and season well with salt and pepper. Arrange the browned meat in a layer. Season again and add the remaining onions, bay leaf, and thyme. Pour in the remaining liquid from the onions and top with remaining potatoes so that they overlap in a single layer. Brush the potatoes with the melted butter and season again.

4 Cover and cook in the preheated oven for 2 hours. Uncover for the last 30 minutes to brown the potatoes. Garnish with chopped herbs and serve immediately with green beans.

FOOD FACT

This classic British dish is named after the old tradition of taking stews to be cooked in the local baker's. To keep the dish hot until lunchtime, the "hotpot" was wrapped in blankets. Dozens of versions claim to be authentic. Some include lamb's kidneys to enrich the gravy, but whatever the ingredients, it is important to season well and cook it slowly.

SHEPHERD'S PIE

INGREDIENTS   Serves 4

2 tbsp. vegetable or olive oil

1 onion, peeled and finely chopped

1 carrot, peeled and finely chopped

1 celery stalk, trimmed and finely chopped

1 tbsp. sprigs of fresh thyme

5 cups finely chopped leftover roast lamb

⅔ cup red wine

⅔ cup lamb or vegetable stock

2 tbsp. tomato paste

salt and freshly ground black pepper

4 cups roughly chopped potatoes

2 tbsp. butter

6 tbsp. milk

1 tbsp. freshly chopped parsley

fresh herbs, to garnish

1 Preheat the oven to 400° F about 15 minutes before cooking. Heat the oil in a large saucepan and add the onion, carrot, and celery. Cook over a medium heat for 8–10 minutes, until softened and starting to brown.

2 Add the thyme and cook briefly, then add the cooked lamb, wine, stock, and tomato paste. Season to taste with salt and pepper, and simmer gently for 25–30 minutes or until reduced and thickened. Remove from the heat to cool slightly and season again.

3 Meanwhile, boil the potatoes in plenty of salted water for 12–15 minutes until tender. Drain and return to the saucepan over a low heat to dry out. Remove from the heat and add the butter, milk, and parsley.

Mash until creamy, adding a little more milk if necessary. Season.

4 Transfer the lamb mixture to a shallow ovenproof dish. Spoon the mashed potatoes over the filling, spreading evenly to cover completely. Fork the surface, then cook in the preheated oven for 25–30 minutes until the potato topping is browned and the filling is piping hot. Garnish and serve.

TASTY TIP

A traditional Shepherd's pie is always made from cold roast lamb, but you can make it with fresh ground lamb if desired. Simply fry 1 lb. lean meat in a nonstick skillet over a high heat until well-browned, then follow the recipe.

CORNISH PASTIES

INGREDIENTS　　　　　　　　　Makes 8

FOR THE PASTRY:
3 cups self-rising flour
⅓ cup butter or margarine
⅓ cup shortening or lard
salt and freshly ground black
　pepper

FOR THE FILLING:
1¼ lbs. braising steak, chopped
　very finely
1 large onion, peeled and

finely chopped
1 large potato, peeled and diced
heaping 1 cup peeled and
　diced rutabaga
3 tbsp. Worcestershire sauce
1 small egg, beaten, to glaze

TO GARNISH:
tomato slices or wedges
sprigs of fresh parsley

1 Preheat the oven to 350° F. To make the pastry, sift the flour into a large bowl and add the fats, chopped into little pieces. Rub the fats and flour together until the mixture resembles coarse bread crumbs. Season to taste with salt and pepper, and mix again.

2 Add about 2 tablespoons of cold water, a little at a time, and mix until the crumbs come together to form a firm, but pliable, dough. Turn onto a lightly floured surface, knead until smooth, then wrap, and chill in the refrigerator.

3 To make the filling, put the braising steak in a large bowl with the onion. Add the potatoes and rutabaga to the bowl, along with the Worcestershire sauce, and salt and pepper. Mix well.

4 Divide the dough into 8 balls and roll each ball into a circle about 10 in. across. Divide the filling among the circles of pastry. Wet the edge of the pastry, then fold over the filling. Pinch the edges to seal.

5 Transfer the pasties to a lightly greased cookie sheet. Make a couple of small holes in each pasty and brush with beaten egg. Cook in the preheated oven for 15 minutes, remove, and brush again with the egg. Return to the oven for an additional 30—40 minutes until golden. Cool slightly, garnish with tomato and parsley, and serve.

TASTY TIP

The pastry for these pasties is made with self-rising flour, which gives it a softer, lighter texture.

SEARED CALF'S LIVER WITH ONIONS & MUSTARD MASH

INGREDIENTS

Serves 2

2 tbsp. olive oil

7 tbsp. butter

3 large onions, peeled and finely sliced

pinch of sugar

salt and freshly ground black pepper

1 tbsp. sprigs of fresh thyme

1 tbsp. balsamic vinegar

4 cups peeled and roughly chopped potatoes

6–8 tbsp. milk

1 tbsp. whole-grain mustard

3–4 fresh sage leaves

1¼ lbs. thinly sliced calf's liver

1 tsp. lemon juice

1 Preheat the oven to 300° F. Heat half the oil and 2 tablespoons of the butter in a flameproof casserole dish. When foaming, add the onions. Cover and cook over a low heat for 20 minutes until softened and beginning to collapse. Add the sugar, and season with salt and pepper. Stir in the thyme. Cover and transfer to the preheated oven. Cook for an additional 30–45 minutes until softened completely, but not browned. Remove from the oven and stir in the balsamic vinegar.

2 Meanwhile, cook the potatoes in salted, boiling water for 15–18 minutes until tender. Drain well, then return to the pan. Place over a low heat to dry completely, remove from the heat, and stir in 4 tablespoons of the butter, the milk, mustard, and salt and pepper to taste. Mash until creamy and keep warm.

3 Heat a large skillet and add the remaining butter and oil. When the fat is foaming, add the mustard and sage leaves, and stir for a few seconds, then add the liver. Cook over a high heat for 1–2 minutes on each side. It should remain slightly pink—do not overcook. Remove the liver from the pan. Add the lemon juice and swirl it around to deglaze the pan.

4 To serve, place a large spoonful of the mashed potatoes on each plate. Top with some of the onions, the liver, and finally the pan juices.

HELPFUL HINT

Calf's liver is mild and tender, and needs only brief cooking over a high heat to sear the outside, but keep it moist and juicy within.

RED WINE RISOTTO WITH LAMB'S KIDNEYS & CARAMELIZED SHALLOTS

INGREDIENTS   Serves 4

8 lamb's kidneys, halved and cores removed

⅔ cup milk

2 tbsp. olive oil

¼ cup butter

¾ lb. shallots, peeled and halved if large

1 onion, peeled and finely chopped

2 garlic cloves, peeled and finely chopped

2 cups Arborio rice

1 cup red wine

4¼ cups chicken or vegetable stock, heated

1 tbsp. sprigs of fresh thyme

½ cup grated Parmesan cheese

salt and freshly ground black pepper

fresh herbs, to garnish

1 Place the lamb's kidneys in a bowl and pour the milk over. Let soak for 15–20 minutes, then drain and pat dry on paper towels. Discard the milk.

2 Heat 1 tablespoon of the oil with half of the butter in a medium saucepan. Add the shallots, cover, and cook for 10 minutes over a gentle heat. Remove the lid and cook for an additional 10 minutes or until tender and golden.

3 Meanwhile, heat the remaining oil with the remaining butter in a deep-sided skillet. Add the onion and cook over a medium heat for 5–7 minutes until starting to brown. Add the garlic and cook briefly.

4 Stir in the rice and cook for a minute until glossy and well coated in oil and butter. Add half the red wine and stir until absorbed. Add a ladleful or two of the stock and stir well until the stock is absorbed. Continue adding the stock, a ladleful at a time, stirring well between additions, until all of it is added and the rice is just tender, but still firm. Remove from the heat.

5 Meanwhile, when the rice is nearly cooked, increase the heat under the shallots, and add the thyme and kidneys. Cook for 3–4 minutes, then add the wine.

6 Bring to a boil, then simmer rapidly until the red wine is reduced and syrupy. Stir the cheese into the rice with the caramelized shallots and kidneys. Season to taste, garnish and serve.

MARINATED LAMB CHOPS WITH GARLIC FRIED POTATOES

INGREDIENTS

Serves 4

4 thick lamb chops
3 tbsp. olive oil
3 cups peeled and diced
  potatoes
6 unpeeled garlic cloves
mixed salad or freshly cooked
  vegetables, to serve

FOR THE MARINADE:
1 small bunch of fresh thyme,
  leaves removed
1 tbsp. freshly chopped
  rosemary
1 tsp. salt
2 garlic cloves, peeled and
  crushed
zest and juice of 1 lemon
2 tbsp. olive oil

1 Trim the chops of any excess fat, wipe with a clean, damp cloth, and set aside. To make the marinade, pound the thyme leaves and rosemary with the salt until pulpy. Add the garlic and continue pounding until crushed. Stir in the lemon zest and juice, and the olive oil.

2 Pour the marinade over the lamb chops, turning them until they are well coated. Cover lightly and marinate in the refrigerator for about 1 hour.

3 Heat the oil in a large nonstick skillet. Add the potatoes and garlic, and cook over a low heat for about 20 minutes, stirring occasionally. Increase the heat and cook for an additional 10–15 minutes until golden. Drain on paper towels, and add salt to taste. Keep the mixture warm.

4 Heat a griddle until almost smoking. Add the lamb chops and cook for 3–4 minutes on each side until golden, but still pink in the middle. Serve with the potatoes and either a mixed salad or freshly cooked vegetables.

TASTY TIP

Marinating the chops not only adds flavor, but it also tenderizes them, due to the acids in the lemon juice. If time allows, marinate the chops for slightly longer. Try other citrus juices in this recipe. Both orange and lime juice would be delicious.

PORK SAUSAGES WITH ONION GRAVY & BEST-EVER MASH

INGREDIENTS

Serves 4

¼ cup butter
1 tbsp. olive oil
2 large onions, peeled and
   thinly sliced
pinch of sugar
1 tbsp. freshly chopped thyme
1 tbsp. all-purpose flour
½ cup Madeira
¾ cup vegetable stock
8–12 good-quality pork
   sausages, depending on size

FOR THE MASHED POTATOES:

2 lbs. floury potatoes, peeled
⅓ cup butter
4 tbsp. crème fraîche or sour
   cream
salt and freshly ground black
   pepper

1 Melt the butter with the oil and add the onions. Cover and cook gently for about 20 minutes until the onions have collapsed. Add the sugar and stir well. Uncover and continue to cook, stirring often, until the onions are very soft and golden. Add the thyme, stir well, then add the flour while stirring. Gradually add the Madeira and the stock. Bring to a boil and simmer gently for 10 minutes.

2 Meanwhile, put the sausages in a large skillet, and cook over a medium heat for about 15–20 minutes, turning often, until golden brown and slightly sticky all over.

3 For the mashed potatoes, boil the potatoes in plenty of lightly salted water for 15–18 minutes until tender. Drain well and return to the saucepan. Put over a low heat to allow to dry. Remove from the heat and add the butter, crème fraîche or sour cream, and salt and pepper. Mash thoroughly. Serve the mashed potatoes topped with the sausages and onion gravy.

HELPFUL HINT

Sausages should always be cooked slowly over a gentle heat to ensure that they are cooked through and evenly browned on the outside. The skins should be slightly crisp and the insides firm. If the sausages are pink on the inside, do not eat them; cook until they are an even color. Serve hot.

CHILI CON CARNE WITH CRISPY-SKINNED POTATOES

INGREDIENTS

Serves 4

2 tbsp. vegetable oil, plus extra for brushing

1 large onion, peeled and finely chopped

1 garlic clove, peeled and finely chopped

1 red chili, deseeded and finely chopped

1 lb. chuck steak, finely chopped, or lean ground beef

1 tbsp. chili powder

14-oz. can chopped tomatoes

2 tbsp. tomato paste

14-oz. can red kidney beans, drained and rinsed

4 large baking potatoes

coarse salt and freshly ground black pepper

TO SERVE:

guacamole

sour cream

1 Preheat the oven to 300° F. Heat the oil in a large flameproof casserole and add the onion. Cook gently for 10 minutes until soft and lightly browned. Add the garlic and chili, and cook briefly. Increase the heat. Add the steak or ground beef and cook for an additional 10 minutes, stirring occasionally, until browned.

2 Add the chili powder and stir well. Cook for about 2 minutes, then add the chopped tomatoes and tomato paste. Bring slowly to a boil. Cover and cook in the preheated oven for 1½ hours.

3 Meanwhile, brush a little vegetable oil all over the potatoes and rub on some coarse salt. Put the potatoes in the oven alongside the chili.

4 To serve, remove the chili from the oven and stir in the kidney beans. Return to the oven for an additional 15 minutes. Cut a cross in each potato, then squeeze to open slightly, and season to taste with salt and pepper. Serve with the chili, guacamole, and sour cream.

TASTY TIP

Make your own guacamole by peeling, pitting, and mashing 1 large avocado in a bowl with 2 tablespoons each of lemon juice and crème fraîche, ¼ teaspoon hot sauce, 1 crushed garlic clove, and salt and pepper. Push the avocado pit into the dip to keep it from discoloring.

ROAST CURED PORK LOIN WITH BAKED, SLICED POTATOES

INGREDIENTS   Serves 4

2 tbsp. whole-grain mustard
2 tbsp. honey
1 tsp. coarsely crushed black
  pepper
2 lb. piece of smoked, cured
  pork loin
5 cups peeled and thinly sliced
  potatoes

⅓ cup butter, diced
1 large onion, peeled and
  finely chopped
¼ cup all-purpose flour
salt and freshly ground black
  pepper
2½ cups milk
fresh green salad, to serve

1 Preheat the oven to 375° F. Mix together the mustard, honey, and black pepper. Spread evenly over the pork loin. Place in the center of a large square of aluminum foil and wrap loosely. Cook in the preheated oven for 15 minutes per pound, plus an additional 15 minutes (total cooking time 45 minutes). Unwrap the joint for the last 30 minutes of cooking time.

2 Meanwhile, layer one third of the potatoes, one third of the butter, half the onions, and half the flour in a large gratin dish. Add half the remaining potatoes and butter, and the remaining onions and flour. Finally, cover with the remaining potatoes. Season well with salt and pepper between layers. Pour in the milk, and dot with the remaining butter. Cover loosely with foil. Put in the oven below the pork. Cook for 1½ hours.

3 Uncover the potatoes and cook for an additional 20 minutes until tender and golden. Remove the pork loin from the oven and let rest for 10 minutes before carving thinly. Serve with the potatoes and a fresh green salad.

HELPFUL HINT

Delicately flavored, smoked, cured pork loin can be found at specialty meat markets. If you are unable to find it, a regular piece of pork loin can be used instead. It usually has a good layer of rind, so remove it for this recipe. Sprinkle with a little salt, and cook separately under the broiler.

GRILLED STEAKS WITH SAFFRON POTATOES & ROAST TOMATOES

INGREDIENTS   Serves 4

1½ lbs. halved new potatoes
few strands of saffron
1¼ cups vegetable or beef
  stock
1 small onion, peeled and
  finely chopped
⅓ cup butter
salt and freshly ground black
  pepper
2 tsp. balsamic vinegar

2 tbsp. olive oil
1 tsp. granulated sugar
8 plum tomatoes, halved
4 boneless steaks, each
  weighing ½ lb.
2 tbsp. freshly chopped
  parsley

1 Cook the potatoes in salted, boiling water for 8 minutes and drain well. Return the potatoes to the saucepan, along with the saffron, stock, onion, and one third of the butter. Season to taste with salt and pepper, and simmer uncovered for 10 minutes until the potatoes are tender.

2 Meanwhile, turn on the broiler. Mix together the vinegar, olive oil, sugar, and seasoning. Arrange the tomatoes cut-side up in a broiler pan lined with aluminum foil, and drizzle over the dressing. Broil for 12–15 minutes, basting occasionally, until tender.

3 Melt the remaining butter in a large skillet. Add the steaks and cook for 4–8 minutes, to taste.

4 Arrange the potatoes and tomatoes on the middles of four serving plates. Top with the steaks, along with any pan juices. Sprinkle over the parsley and serve immediately.

HELPFUL HINT

You can tell how well a steak is cooked by lightly pressing with your fingertips—the less the resistance, the rarer the meat. Timing depends on the thickness rather than the weight of the steak. As a rough guide, a ¾-in. thick steak will take about 2 minutes on each side for rare, 3–4 minutes on each side for medium, and 6–7 minutes on each side for well-done.

OSSO BUCO WITH SAFFRON RISOTTO

INGREDIENTS　　　　　　　　Serves 4

½ cup butter

2 tbsp. olive oil

4 large pieces of veal shank

2 onions, peeled and roughly chopped

2 garlic cloves, peeled and finely chopped

1¼ cups white wine

5 plum tomatoes, peeled and chopped

1 tbsp. tomato paste

salt and freshly ground black pepper

2 tbsp. freshly chopped parsley

grated zest of 1 small lemon

few strands of saffron, crushed

2 cups Arborio rice

5½ cups chicken stock, heated

½ cup grated Parmesan cheese

1 Heat half the butter with half the oil in a large saucepan, and add the pieces of veal. Brown lightly on both sides, then transfer to a plate. Add half the onion and the garlic, and cook gently for about 10 minutes until the onion is just golden.

2 Return the veal to the pan, and add the white wine, tomatoes, and tomato paste. Season lightly with salt and pepper, cover, and bring to a gentle simmer. Cook very gently for 1 hour. Uncover and cook for an additional 30 minutes until the meat is cooked and the sauce is reduced and thickened. Season to taste. Mix together the remaining garlic, parsley, and lemon zest, and set aside.

3 Meanwhile, slowly melt the remaining butter and oil in a large deep-sided skillet. Add the remaining onion and cook gently for 5–7 minutes until just brown. Add the saffron and stir for a few seconds, then add the rice. Cook for an additional minute until the rice is well coated in oil and butter.

4 Begin adding the stock a ladleful at a time, stirring well after each addition and waiting until it is absorbed before adding the next. Continue in this way until all the stock is used. Remove from the heat and stir in the grated Parmesan cheese and seasoning.

5 Spoon a little of the saffron risotto onto each of four serving plates. Top with the osso buco and sauce, and sprinkle with the garlic and parsley mixture. Serve immediately.

SPANISH-STYLE PORK STEW WITH SAFFRON RICE

INGREDIENTS   Serves 4

2 tbsp. olive oil

2 lbs. lean boneless pork, diced

1 large onion, peeled and sliced

2 garlic cloves, peeled and finely chopped

1 tbsp. all-purpose flour

1 lb. plum tomatoes, peeled and chopped

¾ cup red wine

1 tbsp. freshly chopped basil

1 green bell pepper, deseeded and sliced

½ cup pimiento-stuffed olives, cut in half crosswise

salt and freshly ground black pepper

fresh basil leaves, to garnish

FOR THE SAFFRON RICE:

1 tbsp. olive oil

2 tbsp. butter

1 small onion, peeled and finely chopped

few strands of saffron, crushed

1½ cups long-grain white rice

2½ cups chicken stock

1 Preheat the oven to 300° F. Heat the oil in a large flameproof casserole and add the pork in batches. Fry over a high heat until browned. Transfer each batch to a plate until all the pork is browned.

2 Reduce the heat and add the onion to the casserole. Cook for an additional 5 minutes until soft and starting to brown. Add the garlic. Stir briefly before returning the pork to the casserole. Add the flour and stir.

3 Add the tomatoes. Gradually stir in the red wine and add the basil. Bring to simmering point and cover. Transfer the casserole to the lower part of the preheated oven and cook for 1½ hours. Stir in the green pepper and olives, and cook for 30 minutes. Season to taste with salt and pepper.

4 To make the saffron rice, heat the oil with the butter in a saucepan. Add the onion and cook for 5 minutes over a medium heat until softened. Add the saffron and rice, and stir well. Add the stock, bring to a boil, cover, and reduce the heat as much as possible. Cook for 15 minutes, covered, until the rice is tender and the stock is absorbed. Adjust the seasoning and serve with the stew, garnished with fresh basil.

BEEF TERIYAKI WITH GREEN & BLACK RICE

INGREDIENTS
Serves 4

3 tbsp. sake (Japanese rice wine)

3 tbsp. dry sherry

3 tbsp. dark soy sauce

1½ tbsp. brown sugar

4 trimmed steaks, each weighing 6 oz.

2 cups mixed long-grain and wild rice

1-in. piece ginger

½ lb. snow peas

salt

6 scallions, trimmed and cut into fine strips

1 In a small saucepan, gently heat the sake, dry sherry, dark soy sauce, and sugar until the sugar has dissolved. Increase the heat and bring to a boil. Remove from the heat and leave until cold. Lightly wipe the steaks, place in a shallow dish, and pour the sake mixture over. Cover loosely and marinate in the refrigerator for at least 1 hour, spooning the marinade over the steaks occasionally.

2 Cook the rice with the ginger, according to the package's instructions. Drain well, then remove and discard the piece of ginger.

3 Slice the snow peas thinly lengthwise into fine shreds. Plunge into a saucepan of salted, boiling water, return the water to a boil, and drain immediately. Stir the drained snow peas and scallions into the hot rice.

4 Meanwhile, heat a griddle until almost smoking. Remove the steaks from the marinade and cook on the hot griddle for 3–4 minutes each side, depending on the thickness.

5 Place the remaining marinade in a saucepan and bring to a boil. Simmer rapidly for 2 minutes and remove from the heat. When the steaks are cooked as desired, allow to rest for 2–3 minutes, then slice thinly and serve with the rice and the hot marinade.

FOOD FACT

Before 1867, meat was prohibited in Japan to try to prevent aggression. The Japanese still eat a relatively small amount of meat and tend to use quick-cook tender cuts in dishes.

CHICKEN BASQUAISE

INGREDIENTS

Serves 4–6

3 lb. chicken, cut into 8 pieces
2 tbsp. all-purpose flour
salt and freshly ground black
   pepper
3 tbsp. olive oil
1 large onion, peeled and
   sliced
2 red bell peppers, deseeded
   and cut into thick strips
2 garlic cloves, peeled and
   crushed
¼ lb. spicy chorizo sausage,
   cut into ½-in. pieces

heaping 1 cup long-grain
   white rice
2 cups chicken stock
1 tsp. crushed dried chilies
½ tsp. dried thyme
1 tbsp. tomato paste
1¼ cups diced Spanish ham
12 black olives
2 tbsp. freshly chopped
   parsley

1 Dry the chicken pieces well with paper towels. Put the flour in a plastic bag, season with salt and pepper, and add the chicken pieces. Twist the bag to seal, then shake to coat the chicken pieces thoroughly.

2 Heat 2 tablespoons of the oil in a large heavy-based saucepan over a medium-high heat. Add the chicken pieces and cook for about 15 minutes, turning on all sides, until well browned. Using a slotted spoon, transfer to a plate.

3 Add the remaining olive oil to the saucepan, then add the onion and bell peppers. Reduce the heat to medium and cook, stirring frequently, until starting to brown and soften. Stir in the garlic and chorizo, and continue

cooking for an additional 3 minutes. Add the rice and cook for about 2 minutes, stirring to coat with the oil, until the rice is translucent and golden.

4 Stir in the stock, crushed chilies, thyme, tomato paste, and salt and pepper, and bring to a boil. Return the chicken to the saucepan, pressing it gently into the rice. Cover and cook over a very low heat for about 45 minutes until the chicken and rice are cooked and tender.

5 Gently stir in the ham, black olives, and half the parsley. Cover and heat for an additional 5 minutes. Sprinkle with the remaining parsley and serve immediately.

PAD THAI

INGREDIENTS   Serves 4

½ lb. flat rice noodles
2 tbsp. vegetable oil
½ lb. boneless chicken breast, skinned and thinly sliced
4 shallots, peeled and thinly sliced
2 garlic cloves, peeled and finely chopped
4 scallions, trimmed and cut diagonally into 2-in. pieces
¾ lb. fresh white crabmeat or tiny shrimp
1½ cups fresh bean sprouts, rinsed and drained
2 tbsp. preserved or fresh radish, chopped

2–3 tbsp. roasted peanuts, chopped (optional)

FOR THE SAUCE:
3 tbsp. Thai fish sauce
2–3 tbsp. rice vinegar or cider vinegar
1 tbsp. oyster sauce
1 tbsp. toasted sesame oil
1 tbsp. light brown sugar
1 red chili, deseeded and thinly sliced

1 To make the sauce, whisk all the sauce ingredients in a bowl and set aside. Put the rice noodles in a large bowl and pour over enough hot water to cover. Let stand for about 15 minutes until softened. Drain and rinse, then drain again.

2 Heat the oil in a wok over a high heat until hot, but not smoking. Add the chicken strips and stir-fry constantly until they begin to color. Using a slotted spoon, transfer to a plate. Reduce the heat to medium-high.

3 Add the shallots, garlic, and scallions, and stir-fry for 1 minute. Stir in the rice noodles, then the sauce; mix well.

4 Add the chicken strips with the crabmeat, bean sprouts, and radish, and stir well. Cook for about 5 minutes, stirring frequently, until heated through. If the noodles begin to stick, add a little water.

5 Turn into a large shallow serving dish and sprinkle with the chopped peanuts, if desired. Serve immediately.

HELPFUL HINT

Rice noodles are usually sold dried, but fresh noodles are sometimes available. Check package instructions on use.

FRIED GINGER RICE WITH SOY GLAZED DUCK

INGREDIENTS   Serves 4–6

2 duck breasts, skinned and cut diagonally into thin slices
2–3 tbsp. Japanese soy sauce
1 tbsp. mirin (sweet rice wine) or sherry
2 tbsp. brown sugar
2-in. piece of ginger, peeled and finely chopped
4 tbsp. peanut or vegetable oil
2 garlic cloves, peeled and crushed
1¾ cups long-grain brown rice
3¾ cups chicken stock
freshly ground black pepper

⅔ cup diced, lean, cooked ham
1 cup snow peas, cut in half diagonally
8 scallions, trimmed and thinly sliced diagonally
1 tbsp. freshly chopped cilantro
sweet or hot chili sauce, to taste (optional)
sprigs of cilantro, to garnish

1 Put the duck slices in a bowl with 1 tablespoon of the soy sauce, the mirin, 1 teaspoon of the sugar, and one third of the ginger; stir. Set aside.

2 Heat 2 tablespoons of the oil in a large heavy-based saucepan. Add the garlic and half the remaining ginger, and stir-fry for 1 minute. Add the rice and cook for 3 minutes, stirring constantly, until translucent.

3 Stir in all but ½ cup of the stock, along with 1 teaspoon of the soy sauce, and bring to a boil. Season with pepper. Reduce the heat to very low and simmer, covered, for 25–30 minutes until the rice is tender and the liquid is absorbed. Cover and let stand.

4 Heat the remaining oil in a large skillet or wok. Drain the duck strips and add to the frying pan. Stir-fry for 2–3 minutes until just colored. Add 1 tablespoon of soy sauce and the remaining sugar, and cook for 1 minute until glazed. Transfer to a plate and keep warm.

5 Stir in the ham, snow peas, scallions, the remaining ginger, and the chopped cilantro. Add the remaining stock and duck marinade, and cook until the liquid is almost reduced. Fork in the rice and a little chili sauce to taste; stir well. Turn into a serving dish and top with the duck. Garnish with cilantro and serve immediately.

Persian Chicken Pilaf

INGREDIENTS   Serves 4–6

2–3 tbsp. vegetable oil

1½ lbs. boneless skinless chicken pieces (breast and thighs), cut into 1-in. pieces

2 medium onions, peeled and coarsely chopped

1 tsp. ground cumin

heaping 1 cup long-grain white rice

1 tbsp. tomato paste

1 tsp. saffron strands

salt and freshly ground black pepper

1 cup pomegranate juice

3¾ cups chicken stock

1 cup halved and pitted dried apricots or prunes

2 tbsp. raisins

2 tbsp. freshly chopped mint or parsley

pomegranate seeds, to garnish (optional)

1 Heat the oil in a large, heavy-based saucepan over a medium-high heat. Cook the chicken pieces in batches until lightly browned. Return all the browned chicken to the saucepan.

2 Add the onions to the saucepan, reduce the heat to medium, and cook for 3–5 minutes, stirring frequently, until the onions begin to soften. Add the cumin and rice, and stir to coat the rice. Cook for about 2 minutes until the rice is golden and translucent. Stir in the tomato paste and the saffron strands, then season to taste with salt and pepper.

3 Add the pomegranate juice and stock, and bring to a boil, stirring once or twice. Add the apricots and raisins, and stir gently. Reduce the heat to low and cook for 30 minutes until the chicken and rice are tender and the liquid is absorbed.

4 Turn into a shallow serving dish and sprinkle with the chopped mint or parsley. Serve immediately, garnished with pomegranate seeds, if desired.

HELPFUL HINT

Pomegranate juice is available from Middle-Eastern groceries and some specialty stores. You can extract juice from fresh pomegranates by separating the seeds from the bitter pith and membranes, then crushing the seeds in a sieve placed over a bowl. Substitute unsweetened grape or apple juice if you cannot get pomegranates.

CHICKEN & SEAFOOD RISOTTO

INGREDIENTS

Serves 6–8

½ cup olive oil

3 lbs. chicken, cut into 8 pieces

¾ lbs. spicy chorizo sausage, cut into ½-in. pieces

⅔ cup diced cooked ham

1 onion, peeled and chopped

2 red or yellow bell peppers, deseeded and cut into 1-in. pieces

4 garlic cloves, peeled and finely chopped

4⅓ cups short-grain Spanish rice or Arborio rice

2 bay leaves

1 tsp. dried thyme

1 tsp. saffron strands, lightly crushed

¾ cup dry white wine

6½ cups chicken stock

salt and freshly ground black pepper

⅔ cup fresh shelled peas

1 lb. uncooked shrimp

36 clams and/or mussels, well scrubbed

2 tbsp. freshly chopped parsley

TO GARNISH:

lemon wedges

fresh parsley sprigs

1 Heat half the oil in an 18-in. paella pan or deep, wide skillet. Add the chicken pieces and fry for 15 minutes, turning constantly until golden. Remove from the pan and set aside. Add the chorizo and ham to the pan and cook for 6 minutes until crisp, stirring occasionally. Remove and add to the chicken.

2 Add the onion to the pan and cook for 3 minutes or until beginning to soften. Add the peppers and garlic, and cook for 2 minutes; add to the chicken, chorizo, and ham.

3 Add the remaining oil to the pan and stir in the rice until well coated. Stir in the bay leaves, thyme, and saffron, then pour in the wine, and bubble until evaporated. Stir in the stock and bring to a boil, stirring occasionally.

4 Return the chicken, chorizo, ham, and vegetables to the pan, burying them in the rice. Season to taste with salt and pepper. Reduce the heat, and simmer for 10 minutes, stirring occasionally.

5 Add the peas and seafood, pushing them gently into the rice. Cover, and cook over a low heat for 5 minutes, or until the rice and shrimp are tender and the clams and mussels open (discard any that do not open). Let stand for 5 minutes. Sprinkle with the parsley, garnish, and serve.

NEW ORLEANS JAMBALAYA

INGREDIENTS   Serves 6–8

FOR THE SEASONING MIX:
2 dried bay leaves
1 tsp. salt
2 tsp. cayenne pepper
2 tsp. dried oregano
1 tsp. each ground white and
  black pepper, or to taste

3 tbsp. vegetable oil
1¼ cups diced cooked ham
½ lb. smoked pork sausage,
  cut into chunks
2 large onions, peeled and
  chopped
4 celery stalks, trimmed and
  chopped

2 green bell peppers,
  deseeded and chopped
2 garlic cloves, peeled and
  finely chopped
¾ lb. raw chicken, diced
14 oz. can chopped tomatoes
2½ cups fish stock
2⅓ cups long-grain white rice
4 scallions, trimmed and
  coarsely chopped
¾ lb. raw shrimp, peeled
½ lb. white crabmeat

1 Mix all the seasoning ingredients together in a small bowl and set aside.

2 Heat 2 tablespoons of the oil in a large flameproof casserole over a medium heat. Add the ham and sausage, and cook, stirring often, for 7–8 minutes until golden. Remove from the pan and set aside.

3 Add the remaining onions, celery, and peppers to the casserole and cook for about 4 minutes or until softened, stirring occasionally. Stir in the garlic, then, using a slotted spoon, transfer all the vegetables to a plate and set aside with the sausage.

4 Add the chicken pieces to the casserole and cook for about 4 minutes or until beginning to brown, turning once. Stir in the seasoning mix and turn the pieces to coat well. Return the sausage and vegetables to the casserole and stir well. Add the chopped tomatoes with their juice and the stock, and bring to a boil.

5 Stir in the rice and reduce the heat to low. Cover and simmer for 12 minutes. Uncover, stir in the scallions and shrimp, and cook, covered, for an additional 4 minutes. Add the crab and gently stir in. Cook for 2–3 minutes or until the rice is tender. Remove from the heat, cover, and let stand for 5 minutes before serving.

RICE-STUFFED POUSSINS

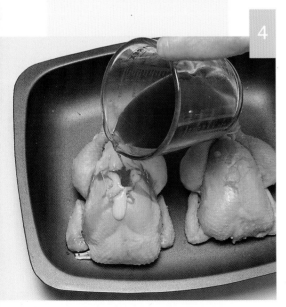

INGREDIENTS   Serves 6

FOR THE RICE STUFFING:

1 cup port

¾ cup raisins

1 cup chopped dried apricots

2 tbsp. olive oil

1 medium onion, peeled and finely chopped

1 celery stalk, trimmed and finely sliced

2 garlic cloves, peeled and finely chopped

1½ tsp. mixed spice

1 tsp. each dried oregano and mint or basil

2 cups chopped, unsweetened, canned chestnuts

heaping 1 cup cooked long-grain white rice

grated zest and juice of 2 oranges

1½ cups chicken stock

½ cup lightly toasted and chopped walnut halves

2 tbsp. each freshly chopped mint and parsley

salt and freshly ground black pepper

6 oven-ready game hens

¼ cup butter, melted

TO GARNISH:

fresh herbs

orange wedges

1 Preheat the oven to 350° F. For the stuffing, place the port, raisins, and apricots in a bowl and let stand for 15 minutes. In an oiled pan, add the onion and celery, and cook for 3–4 minutes. Add the garlic, mixed spices, herbs, and chestnuts, and cook for 4 minutes, stirring often. Add the rice, half the orange zest and juice, and the stock. Simmer for 5 minutes until the liquid is absorbed.

2 Drain the raisins and apricots, setting aside the port. Stir into the rice with the walnuts, mint, parsley, and seasoning, and cook for 2 minutes. Remove.

3 Rinse the game hen cavities, pat dry, and season with salt and pepper. Lightly fill the cavities with the stuffing. Tie the legs together, tucking in the tails. Form extra stuffing into balls.

4 Place in roasting pan with stuffing balls, and brush with melted butter. Drizzle over the remaining butter, remaining orange zest and juice, and port. Roast in the preheated oven for 50 minutes or until golden and cooked, basting every 15 minutes. Transfer to a platter, cover with foil, and rest. Pour over any pan juices. Garnish with herbs and orange wedges. Serve with the stuffing.

CREAMY CHICKEN & RICE PILAF

INGREDIENTS   Serves 4–6

2 cups basmati rice
salt and freshly ground black
  pepper
¼ cup butter
1 cup flaked almonds
⅔ cup unsalted shelled
  pistachio nuts
4–6 skinless chicken breast
  fillets, each cut into 4 pieces
2 tbsp. vegetable oil
2 medium onions, peeled and
  thinly sliced
2 garlic cloves, peeled and
  finely chopped
1-in. piece of ginger, finely
  chopped

6 green cardamom pods,
  lightly crushed
4–6 whole cloves
2 bay leaves
1 tsp. ground coriander
½ tsp. cayenne pepper, or to
  taste
1 cup plain yogurt
1 cup heavy cream
½ lb. seedless green grapes,
  halved if large
2 tbsp. freshly chopped
  cilantro or mint

1 Bring a saucepan of lightly salted water to a boil. Pour in the rice, return to boil, then simmer for about 12 minutes until tender. Drain, rinse under cold water, and set aside.

2 Heat the butter in a large deep skillet over a medium-high heat. Add the almonds and pistachios, and cook for about 2 minutes, stirring constantly, until golden. Using a slotted spoon, transfer to a plate.

3 Add the chicken pieces to the pan and cook for 5 minutes or until golden, turning once. Remove from the pan and set aside. Add the oil to the pan. Cook the onions for 10 minutes

or until golden, stirring frequently. Stir in the garlic, ginger, and spices, and cook for 2–3 minutes, stirring.

4 Add 2–3 tablespoons of the yogurt, and cook, stirring, until the moisture evaporates. Continue adding the yogurt in this way until it is used up.

5 Return the chicken and nuts to the pan and stir. Stir in ½ cup of boiling water, and season to taste with salt and pepper. Cook, covered, over a low heat for 10 minutes, until the chicken is tender. Stir in the cream, grapes, and half the herbs. Gently fold in the rice. Heat for 5 minutes, sprinkle with herbs, then serve.

WILD RICE & BACON SALAD WITH SMOKED CHICKEN

INGREDIENTS   Serves 4

heaping ¾ cup wild rice
½ cup pecan or walnut halves
1 tbsp. vegetable oil
4 slices smoked bacon, diced
3–4 shallots, peeled and finely
   chopped
5 tbsp. walnut oil

2–3 tbsp. sherry or cider
   vinegar
2 tbsp. freshly chopped dill
salt and freshly ground black
   pepper
1⅓ cups thinly sliced smoked
   chicken or duck breast
dill sprigs, to garnish

1 Put the wild rice in a medium saucepan with 2½ cups water and bring to a boil, stirring once or twice. Reduce the heat, cover, and simmer gently for 30–50 minutes, depending on the texture you prefer, chewy or tender. Using a fork, gently fluff into a large bowl and allow to cool slightly.

2 Meanwhile, toast the nuts in a skillet over a medium heat for 2 minutes or until they are fragrant and lightly colored, stirring and tossing frequently. Cool, then chop coarsely, and add to the rice.

3 Heat the oil in the skillet over a medium heat. Add the bacon and cook, stirring from time to time, for 3–4 minutes or until crisp and brown. Remove from the pan and drain on paper towels. Add the shallots to the pan and cook for 4 minutes or until just softened, stirring from

time to time. Stir into the rice and nuts, along with the drained bacon pieces.

4 Whisk the walnut oil, vinegar, half the dill, and salt and pepper in a small bowl until combined. Pour the dressing over the rice mixture and toss well to combine. Mix the chicken and the remaining chopped dill into the rice, then spoon into bowls and garnish each serving with a dill sprig. Serve slightly warm or at room temperature.

FOOD FACT

Both smoked chicken and duck have a delicate smoky flavor which comes from being first cold-smoked, then briefly hot-smoked. You can, of course, use plain roasted chicken or duck if desired.

CHICKEN & WHITE WINE RISOTTO

INGREDIENTS   Serves 4–6

2 tbsp. oil
½ cup butter
2 shallots, peeled and finely
  chopped
1¾ cups Arborio rice
2½ cups dry white wine
3¼ cups chicken stock, heated
¾ lb. skinless chicken breast
  fillets, thinly sliced
½ cup grated Parmesan cheese

2 tbsp. freshly chopped dill or
  parsley
salt and freshly ground black
  pepper

1 Heat the oil and half the butter in a large heavy-based saucepan over a medium-high heat. Add the shallots and cook for 2 minutes or until softened, stirring frequently. Add the rice and cook for 2–3 minutes, stirring frequently, until the rice is translucent and well coated.

2 Pour in half the wine; it will bubble and steam rapidly. Cook, stirring constantly, until the liquid is absorbed. Add a ladleful of the hot stock and cook until the liquid is absorbed. Carefully stir in the chicken.

3 Continue adding the stock, about half a ladleful at a time, allowing each addition to be absorbed before adding the next; never allow the rice to cook dry. This process should take about 20 minutes. The risotto should have a creamy consistency, and the rice should be tender, but firm to the bite.

4 Stir in the remaining wine and cook for 2–3 minutes. Remove from the heat and stir in the remaining butter with the Parmesan cheese and half the chopped herbs. Season to taste with salt and pepper. Spoon into warmed shallow bowls and sprinkle each with the remaining chopped herbs. Serve immediately.

HELPFUL HINT

Keep the stock to be added to the risotto at a low simmer in a separate saucepan, so that it is piping hot when added to the rice. This will ensure that the dish is kept at a constant heat during cooking, which is important to achieve a perfect creamy texture.

POTATO-STUFFED ROAST POUSSIN

INGREDIENTS   Serves 4

4 oven-ready game hens
salt and freshly ground black
  pepper
1 lemon, cut into quarters
1 lb. floury potatoes, peeled
  and cut into 1½-in. pieces
1 tbsp. freshly chopped thyme
  or rosemary
3–4 tbsp. olive oil

4 garlic cloves, unpeeled and
  lightly smashed
8 slices bacon or prosciutto
  ham
½ cup white wine
2 scallions, trimmed and thinly
  sliced
2 tbsp. heavy cream or crème
  fraîche
lemon wedges, to garnish

1 Preheat the oven to 425° F. Place a roasting pan in the oven to heat. Rinse the cavities of the game hens and pat dry with paper towels. Season the cavities with salt and pepper, and a squeeze of lemon. Push a lemon quarter into each cavity.

2 Put the potatoes in a saucepan of lightly salted water and bring to a boil. Reduce the heat to low and simmer until just tender; do not overcook. Drain and cool slightly. Sprinkle the chopped herbs over the potatoes, and drizzle with 2–3 tablespoons of the oil.

3 Spoon half the seasoned potatoes into the game hen cavities; do not pack too tightly. Rub each hen with a little more oil, and season with pepper. Carefully spoon 1 tablespoon of oil into the hot roasting pan and arrange the game hens in the pan. Spoon the remaining potatoes

around the edge. Sprinkle over the garlic.

4 Roast the hens in the preheated oven for 30 minutes, or until the skin is golden and beginning to crisp. Carefully lay the bacon slices over the breast of each hen, and continue to roast for 15–20 minutes until the hens are cooked through and crisp.

5 Transfer the game hens and potatoes to a serving platter and cover loosely with aluminum foil. Skim off the fat from the juices. Place the pan over a medium heat, and add the wine and scallions. Cook briefly, scraping the bits from the bottom of the pan. Whisk in the cream or crème fraîche, and bubble for 1 minute or until thickened. Garnish the hens with lemon wedges, and serve with the creamy gravy.

Turkey Hash with Potatoes & Beets

INGREDIENTS   Serves 4–6

2 tbsp. vegetable oil
¼ cup butter
4 slices bacon, diced or sliced
1 medium onion, peeled and
   finely chopped
2¼ cups diced cooked turkey
2½ cups finely chopped cooked
   potatoes

2–3 tbsp. freshly chopped
   parsley
2 tbsp. all-purpose flour
1¾ cups diced, cooked beets
green salad, to serve

1 In a large, heavy-based skillet, heat the oil and half the butter over a medium heat until sizzling. Add the bacon and cook for 4 minutes or until crisp and golden, stirring occasionally. Using a slotted spoon, transfer to a large bowl. Add the onion to the pan and cook for 3–4 minutes or until soft and golden, stirring frequently.

2 Meanwhile, add the turkey, potatoes, parsley, and flour to the cooked bacon in the bowl. Stir and toss gently, then fold in the diced beet.

3 Add half the remaining butter to the skillet and then the turkey-vegetable mixture. Stir, then spread the mixture to evenly cover the bottom of the pan. Cook for 15 minutes or until the underside is crisp and brown, pressing the hash firmly with a spatula. Remove from the heat.

4 Place a large plate over the skillet and, holding the plate and pan together with an oven mitt, invert the hash out onto the plate. Heat the remaining butter in the pan, slide the hash back into the pan, and cook for 4 minutes or until crisp and brown on the other side. Invert onto the plate again and serve immediately with a green salad.

TASTY TIP

A hash is usually made just with potatoes, but here they are combined with ruby red beets, which add vibrant color and a sweet earthy flavor to the dish. Make sure that you buy plain beets, rather than the pickled variety.

CHICKEN & NEW POTATOES ON ROSEMARY SKEWERS

INGREDIENTS   Serves 4

8 thick, fresh rosemary stems, at least 9 in. long	4 skinless chicken breast fillets
3–4 tbsp. extra-virgin olive oil	16 small new potatoes, peeled or scrubbed
2 garlic cloves, peeled and crushed	8 very small onions or shallots, peeled
1 tsp. freshly chopped thyme	1 large yellow or red bell pepper, deseeded
grated zest and juice of 1 lemon	lemon wedges, to garnish
salt and freshly ground black pepper	parsley-flavored cooked rice, to serve

1 Preheat the broiler and line the broiler pan with aluminum foil just before cooking. If using a barbecue, light at least 20 minutes before needed. Strip the leaves from the rosemary stems, leaving about 2 in. of soft leaves at the top. Chop the leaves coarsely and set aside. Using a sharp knife, cut the thicker, woody ends of the stems to a sharp point for piercing the chicken and potatoes. Blend the chopped rosemary, oil, garlic, thyme, and lemon zest and juice in a shallow dish. Season to taste with salt and pepper.

2 Cut the chicken into ½-in. cubes, add to the flavored oil, and stir well. Cover, and refrigerate for at least 30 minutes, turning occasionally.

3 Cook the potatoes in lightly salted, boiling water for

10–12 minutes until just tender. Add the onions to the potatoes 2 minutes before the end of the cooking time. Drain, rinse under cold running water, and let cool. Cut the pepper into 1-in. squares.

4 Beginning with a piece of chicken and starting with the pointed end of the skewer, alternately thread equal amounts of chicken, potato, pepper, and onion onto each rosemary skewer. Cover the leafy ends of the skewers with foil to keep them from burning. Do not thread the chicken and vegetables too closely together on the skewer or the chicken may not cook completely.

5 Cook the kabobs for 15 minutes or until tender and golden, turning and brushing with either extra oil or the marinade. Remove the foil, garnish with lemon wedges, and serve on rice.

AROMATIC DUCK PATTIES ON POTATO PANCAKES

INGREDIENTS   Serves 4

1½ lbs. boneless duck breasts
2 tbsp. hoisin sauce
1 garlic clove, peeled and
  finely chopped
4 scallions, trimmed and finely
  chopped
2 tbsp. Japanese soy sauce
½ tsp. Chinese five-spice
  powder
salt and freshly ground black
  pepper

freshly chopped cilantro, to
  garnish
extra hoisin sauce, to serve

FOR THE POTATO PANCAKES:
1 lb. floury potatoes
1 small onion, peeled and
  grated
1 small egg, beaten
1 heaping tbsp. all-purpose
  flour

1 Peel off the thick layer of skin and fat from the duck breasts, and cut into small pieces. Put in a small dry saucepan, and set over a low heat for 10–15 minutes or until the fat runs clear and the crackling goes crisp. Set aside.

2 Cut the duck meat into pieces and blend in a food processor until coarsely chopped. Spoon into a bowl and add the hoisin sauce, garlic, half the scallions, soy sauce, and Chinese five-spice powder. Season to taste with salt and pepper, and shape into 4 patties. Cover and chill in the refrigerator for 1 hour.

3 To make the potato pancakes, shred the potatoes into a large bowl, squeeze out the water with your hands, then put on a clean dishtowel. Twist the ends to squeeze out any remaining water.

Return the potato to the bowl, add the onion and egg, and mix well. Add the flour and salt and pepper. Stir to blend.

4 Heat about 2 tablespoons of the duck fat in a large skillet. Spoon the potato mixture into 2–4 patty shapes, and cook for 6 minutes or until golden and crisp, turning once. Keep warm in the oven. Repeat with the remaining mixture, adding duck fat as needed.

5 Preheat the broiler and line the pan with aluminum foil. Brush the patties with a little of the duck fat and broil for 6–8 minutes, longer if desired, turning once. Arrange 1–2 potato pancakes on a plate and top with a patty. Spoon over a little hoisin sauce, and garnish with the remaining scallions and cilantro.

CHICKEN PIE WITH SWEET POTATO TOPPING

INGREDIENTS   Serves 4

4 cups peeled and coarsely
  diced sweet potatoes
1⅓ cups peeled and coarsely
  diced potatoes
salt and freshly ground black
  pepper
⅔ cup milk
2 tbsp. butter
2 tsp. brown sugar
grated zest of 1 orange
4 skinless chicken breast
  fillets, diced

1 medium onion, peeled and
  coarsely chopped
¼ lb. baby mushrooms, stems
  trimmed
2 leeks, trimmed and thickly
  sliced
⅔ cup dry white wine
1 chicken bouillon cube
1 tbsp. freshly chopped parsley
¼ cup crème fraîche or thick
  heavy cream
green vegetables, to serve

1 Preheat the oven to 375° F. Cook the sweet and regular potatoes together in lightly salted, boiling water until tender. Drain well, then return to the saucepan, and mash until creamy, gradually adding the milk, then the butter, sugar, and orange zest. Season to taste and set aside.

2 Place the chicken in a saucepan with the onion, mushrooms, leeks, wine, bouillon cube, and seasoning to taste. Simmer covered until the chicken and vegetables are tender. Using a slotted spoon, transfer the chicken and vegetables to a pie dish. Add the parsley and crème fraîche to the liquid in the pan, and bring to a boil. Simmer until thickened and smooth, stirring constantly. Pour over the chicken in the pie dish, mix, and cool.

3 Spread the mashed potatoes over the chicken filling, and swirl the surface into decorative peaks. Bake in the preheated oven for 35 minutes or until the top is golden and the chicken is heated through. Serve immediately with fresh green vegetables.

HELPFUL HINT

There are two types of sweet potatoes; one has a cream-colored flesh, the other orange. Both are good for mashing, as in this recipe, but the cream-colored variety has a drier texture, so you may need a little more milk.

WARM CHICKEN & POTATO SALAD WITH PEAS & MINT

INGREDIENTS

Serves 4–6

1 lb. new potatoes, peeled or scrubbed and cut into bite-sized pieces

salt and freshly ground black pepper

2 tbsp. cider vinegar

1¼ cups frozen peas, thawed

1 small ripe avocado

4 cooked chicken breasts, about 1 lb. in weight, skinned and diced

2 tbsp. freshly chopped mint

2 heads romaine lettuce
fresh mint sprigs, to garnish

FOR THE DRESSING:

2 tbsp. raspberry or sherry vinegar

2 tsp. Dijon mustard

1 tsp. honey

¼ cup sunflower oil

¼ cup extra-virgin olive oil

1 Cook the potatoes in lightly salted, boiling water for 15 minutes or until just tender when pierced with the tip of a sharp knife; do not overcook. Rinse under cold running water to cool slightly, then drain and turn into a large bowl. Sprinkle with the cider vinegar and toss gently.

2 Run the peas under hot water to ensure that they are thawed, pat dry with paper towels, and add to the potatoes.

3 Cut the avocado in half lengthwise and remove the pit. Peel and cut the avocado into cubes, and add to the potatoes and peas. Add the chicken and stir together lightly.

4 To make the dressing, place all the ingredients in a screw-top jar with a little salt and pepper. Shake well to mix; add a little more oil if the flavor is too sharp. Pour over the salad and toss gently to coat. Sprinkle in half the mint and stir lightly.

5 Separate the lettuce leaves and spread onto a large shallow serving plate. Spoon the salad on top and sprinkle with the remaining mint. Garnish with mint sprigs and serve.

FOOD FACT

Cider vinegar, made from cider as the name suggests, has a strong, sharp flavor with a hint of apples. Raspberry vinegar has a wine-vinegar base, macerated with fresh raspberries.

BROWN RICE & LENTIL SALAD WITH DUCK

INGREDIENTS

Serves 6

1¼ cups Puy lentils, rinsed

4 tbsp. olive oil

1 medium onion, peeled and finely chopped

1¼ cups long-grain brown rice

½ tsp. dried thyme

2 cups chicken stock

salt and freshly ground black pepper

¾ lb. shiitake or portabella mushrooms, trimmed and sliced

¾ lb. cooked Chinese-style spicy duck or roasted duck, sliced into large chunks

2 garlic cloves, peeled and finely chopped

1¼ cups diced, cooked, smoked ham

2 small zucchini, trimmed, diced, and blanched

6 scallions, trimmed and thinly sliced

2 tbsp. freshly chopped parsley

2 tbsp. walnut halves, toasted and chopped

FOR THE DRESSING:

2 tbsp. red or white wine vinegar

1 tbsp. balsamic vinegar

1 tsp. Dijon mustard

1 tsp. honey

⅓ cup extra-virgin olive oil

2–3 tbsp. walnut oil

1 Bring a large saucepan of water to a boil, sprinkle in the lentils, return to a boil, then simmer over a low heat for 30 minutes, or until tender; do not overcook. Drain and rinse under cold running water, then drain again, and set aside.

2 Heat 2 tablespoons of the oil in a saucepan. Add the onion and cook for 2 minutes until it begins to soften. Stir in the rice with the thyme and stock. Season to taste with salt and pepper, and bring to a boil. Cover and simmer for 40 minutes or until tender and the liquid is absorbed.

3 Heat the remaining oil in a large skillet and add the mushrooms. Cook for 5 minutes until golden. Stir in the duck and garlic, and cook for 2–3 minutes to heat through. Season well.

4 To make the dressing, whisk the vinegars, mustard, and honey in a large serving bowl, then gradually whisk in the oils. Add the lentils and the rice, then stir lightly together. Gently stir in the ham, blanched zucchini, scallions, and parsley. Season to taste and sprinkle with the walnuts. Serve topped with the duck and mushrooms.

CHINESE-STYLE FRIED RICE

INGREDIENTS

Serves 4–6

2–3 tbsp. peanut oil or vegetable oil

2 small onions, peeled and cut into wedges

2 garlic cloves, peeled and thinly sliced

1-in. piece of ginger, peeled and cut into thin slivers

2½ cups shredded, cooked chicken

1¼ cups shredded, cooked ham

1⅓ cups long-grain white rice, cooked and cooled

½ cup canned water chestnuts, sliced

1½ cups cooked peeled shrimp

3 large eggs

3 tsp. sesame oil

salt and freshly ground black pepper

6 scallions, trimmed and sliced into ½-in. pieces

2 tbsp. dark soy sauce

1 tbsp. sweet chili sauce

2 tbsp. freshly chopped cilantro

TO GARNISH:

2 tbsp. chopped roasted peanuts

sprig of fresh cilantro

1 Heat a wok or large deep skillet until very hot, add the oil, and heat for 30 seconds. Add the onions and stir-fry for 2 minutes. Stir in the garlic and ginger, and cook for 1 minute. Add the cooked chicken and ham, and stir-fry for an additional 2–3 minutes.

2 Add the rice, water chestnuts, and shrimp, if using, with 2 tablespoons of water, and stir-fry for 2 minutes until the rice is heated through.

3 Beat the eggs with 1 teaspoon of the sesame oil, and season to taste with salt and pepper. Make a well in the center of the rice, then pour in the egg mixture and stir immediately, gradually drawing the rice mixture into the egg until the egg is cooked.

4 Add the scallions, soy and chili sauces, cilantro, and a little water, if necessary. Adjust the seasoning and drizzle with the remaining sesame oil. Sprinkle with the nuts and serve.

HELPFUL HINT

Long-grain white rice absorbs about 3 times its weight during cooking, so if cooking rice specially for this dish you will need 8 oz. raw rice. Add extra flavor by cooking in vegetable or chicken stock.

TURKEY & PESTO RICE ROULADES

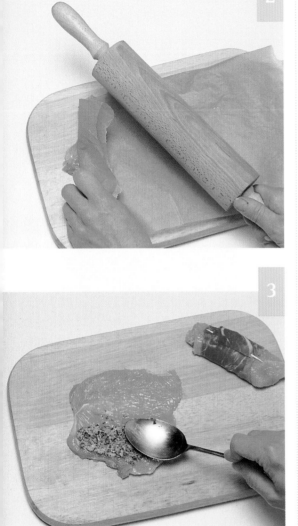

INGREDIENTS   Serves 4

cooked white rice, at room
temperature
1 garlic clove, peeled and
crushed
1–2 tbsp. grated Parmesan
cheese
2 tbsp. prepared pesto sauce
2 tbsp. pine nuts, lightly
toasted and chopped
4 turkey steaks, each weighing
about 5 oz.

salt and freshly ground black
pepper
4 slices prosciutto
2 tbsp. olive oil
¼ cup white wine
2 tbsp. butter, chilled

TO SERVE:
freshly cooked spinach
freshly cooked pasta

1 Put the rice in a bowl and add the garlic, Parmesan cheese, pesto, and pine nuts. Stir to combine the ingredients, then set aside.

2 Place the turkey steaks on a chopping board and, using a sharp knife, slice horizontally through each steak, without cutting all the way through. Fold back the top slice and cover with baking parchment. Flatten slightly by pounding with a meat mallet or rolling pin.

3 Season each steak with salt and pepper. Divide the stuffing equally among the steaks, spreading evenly over one half. Fold the steaks in half to enclose the filling, then wrap each steak in a slice of prosciutto and secure with wooden toothpicks.

4 Heat the oil in a large skillet over medium heat. Cook the steaks for 5 minutes or until golden on one side. Turn and cook for an additional 2 minutes. Push the steaks to the side and pour in the wine. Allow the wine to bubble and evaporate. Add the butter a little at a time, whisking constantly until the sauce is smooth. Discard the toothpicks, then serve the steaks, drizzled with the sauce, with spinach and pasta.

FOOD FACT

Prosciutto, the classic Italian ham, is dry-cured, rubbed with salt for about a month, then hung up to dry for a year. Carved very thinly, it's often served raw, but is also good when lightly fried.

SLOW-ROAST CHICKEN WITH POTATOES & OREGANO

INGREDIENTS

Serves 6

3–4 lb. oven-ready chicken
1 lemon, halved
1 onion, peeled and quartered
¼ cup butter, softened
salt and freshly ground black
  pepper
2¼ lb. potatoes, peeled and
  quartered

3–4 tbsp. extra-virgin olive oil
1 tbsp. dried oregano,
  crumbled
1 tsp. fresh thyme leaves
2 tbsp. freshly chopped thyme
fresh sage leaves, to garnish

1 Preheat the oven to 400° F. Rinse the chicken and dry well, inside and out, with paper towels. Rub the chicken all over with the lemon halves, then squeeze the juice over it and into the cavity. Put the squeezed halves into the cavity with the quartered onion.

2 Rub the softened butter all over the chicken, and season to taste with salt and pepper, then put it in a large roasting pan, breast-side down.

3 Toss the potatoes in the oil, season with salt and pepper to taste, and add the oregano and fresh thyme. Arrange the potatoes, along with the oil, around the chicken, and carefully pour ⅔ cup water into one end of the pan (not over the oil).

4 Roast in the preheated oven for 25 minutes. Reduce the oven temperature to 375° F, and turn the chicken breast-side up. Turn the potatoes, sprinkle with half the fresh herbs, and baste the chicken and potatoes with the juices. Continue roasting for 1 hour or until the chicken is cooked, basting occasionally. If the liquid evaporates completely, add a little more water. The chicken is cooked when the juices run clear when the thigh is pierced with a skewer.

5 Transfer the chicken to a carving dish and let rest for 5 minutes, covered with aluminum foil. Meanwhile, return the potatoes to the oven.

6 Carve the chicken into serving pieces and arrange on a large, heatproof serving dish. Arrange the potatoes around the chicken and drizzle over any remaining juices. Sprinkle with the remaining herbs and serve.

LEEK & POTATO TART

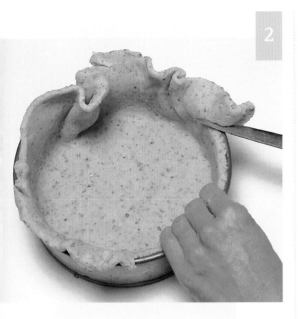

INGREDIENTS   Serves 6

2 cups all-purpose flour
pinch of salt
⅔ cup butter, cubed
½ cup very finely chopped
  walnuts
1 large egg yolk

FOR THE FILLING:
1 lb. leeks, trimmed and thinly
  sliced
3 tbsp. butter

1 lb. large new potatoes,
  scrubbed
1¼ cups sour cream
3 medium eggs, lightly beaten
1½ cups shredded Gruyère
  cheese
freshly grated nutmeg
salt and freshly ground black
  pepper
fresh chives, to garnish

1 Preheat the oven to 400° F. Sift the flour and salt into a bowl. Rub in the butter until the mixture resembles bread crumbs. Stir in the nuts. Mix together the egg yolk and 3 tablespoons of cold water. Sprinkle over the dry ingredients. Mix to form a dough.

2 Knead on a lightly floured surface for a few seconds, then wrap in plastic wrap and chill in the refrigerator for 20 minutes. Roll out and use to line an 8-in. springform pan or very deep tart pan. Chill for an additional 30 minutes.

3 Cook the leeks in the butter over a high heat for 2–3 minutes, stirring constantly. Lower the heat, cover, and cook for 25 minutes until soft, stirring occasionally. Remove the leeks from the heat.

4 Cook the potatoes in boiling salted water for 15 minutes or until almost tender. Drain and slice thickly. Add to the leeks. Stir the sour cream into the leeks and potatoes, followed by the eggs, cheese, nutmeg, and salt and pepper. Pour into the pastry shell, and bake on the middle shelf in the preheated oven for 20 minutes.

5 Reduce the oven temperature to 375° F, and cook for an additional 30–35 minutes or until the filling is set. Garnish with chives and serve immediately.

TASTY TIP

Flavor the pastry with different nuts, such as hazelnuts or almonds, or replace the nuts with 3 tablespoons of freshly chopped mixed herbs.

POTATO GNOCCHI WITH PESTO SAUCE

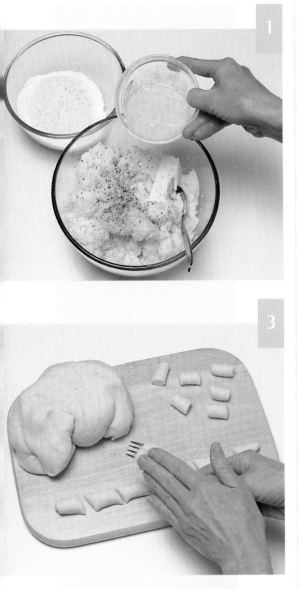

INGREDIENTS

Serves 6

2 lbs. floury potatoes
3 tbsp. butter
1 medium egg, beaten
2 cups all-purpose flour
1 tsp. salt
freshly ground black pepper
⅓ cup shaved Parmesan
  cheese
arugula salad, to serve

FOR THE PESTO SAUCE:
packed 2 cups fresh basil
  leaves
1 large garlic clove, peeled
2 tbsp. pine nuts
½ cup olive oil
⅓ cup grated Parmesan cheese

1 Cook the potatoes in their skins in boiling water for 20 minutes or until tender. Drain and peel. While still warm, push the potatoes through a fine sieve into a bowl. Stir in the butter, egg, 1½ cups of the flour, and the salt and pepper.

2 Sift the remaining flour onto a board or work surface, and add the potato mixture. Gently knead in enough flour to form a soft, slightly sticky dough.

3 With floured hands, break off portions of the dough and roll into 1-in.-thick ropes. Cut into ¾-in. lengths. Lightly press each piece against the inner prongs of a fork. Put on a baking sheet covered with a floured dishtowel, and chill in the refrigerator for about 30 minutes.

4 To make the pesto sauce, put the basil, garlic, pine nuts, and oil in a processor, and blend until smooth and creamy. Turn into a bowl and stir in the Parmesan cheese. Season to taste.

5 Cooking in several batches, drop the gnocchi into a saucepan of barely simmering salted water. Cook for 3–4 minutes or until they float to the surface. Remove with a slotted spoon and keep warm in a covered, greased baking dish in a low oven.

6 Add the gnocchi to the pesto sauce and toss gently to coat. Serve immediately, sprinkled with the Parmesan cheese and accompanied by an arugula salad.

HELPFUL HINT

Use a vegetable peeler to pare the Parmesan cheese into thin, decorative curls.

VEGETARIAN CASSOULET

INGREDIENTS   Serves 4

1⅓ cups dried kidney beans,
  soaked overnight
2 medium onions
1 bay leaf
6¼ cups cold water
2¾ cups peeled and thickly
  sliced potatoes
salt and freshly ground black
  pepper
5 tsp. olive oil
1 large garlic clove, peeled
  and crushed
2 leeks, trimmed and sliced
7-oz. can chopped tomatoes

1 tsp. dark brown sugar
1 tbsp. freshly chopped thyme
2 tbsp. freshly chopped
  parsley
3 zucchini, trimmed and sliced

FOR THE TOPPING:
1 cup fresh white bread
  crumbs
¼ cup finely shredded cheddar
  cheese

1 Preheat the oven to 350° F. Drain the beans, rinse under cold running water, and put in a saucepan. Peel one of the onions and add to the beans with the bay leaf. Pour in the water.

2 Bring to a rapid boil and cook for 10 minutes, then turn down the heat, cover, and simmer for 50 minutes or until the beans are almost tender. Drain the beans, setting aside the liquid, but discarding the onion and bay leaf.

3 Cook the potatoes in a saucepan of lightly salted boiling water for 6–7 minutes, until almost tender when tested with the point of a knife. Drain and set aside.

4 Peel and chop the remaining onion. Heat the oil in a skillet and cook the onion with the garlic and leeks for 10 minutes until softened. Stir in the tomatoes, sugar, thyme, and parsley. Stir in the beans with 1¼ cups of the liquid and season to taste. Simmer uncovered for 5 minutes.

5 Layer the potato slices, zucchini, and ladlefuls of the bean mixture in a large flameproof casserole dish. To make the topping, mix together the bread crumbs and cheese, and sprinkle over the top.

6 Bake in the preheated oven for 40 minutes or until the vegetables are cooked through, and the topping is golden brown and crisp. Serve immediately.

SWEET POTATO PATTIES WITH MANGO & TOMATO SALSA

INGREDIENTS

Serves 4

4 cups peeled and coarsely
 diced sweet potatoes
salt and freshly ground black
 pepper
2 tbsp. butter
1 onion, peeled and chopped
1 garlic clove, peeled and
 crushed
pinch of freshly grated
 nutmeg
1 medium egg, beaten
⅓ cup quick-cook polenta
2 tbsp. sunflower oil

FOR THE SALSA:
1 ripe mango, peeled, pitted,
 and diced
6 cherry tomatoes, cut in
 wedges
4 scallions, trimmed and thinly
 sliced
1 red chili, deseeded and
 finely chopped
finely grated zest and juice of
 ½ lime
2 tbsp. freshly chopped mint
1 tsp. honey
lettuce, to serve

1 Steam or cook the sweet potatoes in lightly salted, boiling water for 15–20 minutes until tender. Drain well, then mash until smooth.

2 Melt the butter in a saucepan. Add the onion and garlic, and cook gently for 10 minutes until soft. Add to the mashed sweet potatoes, and season with the nutmeg, salt, and pepper. Stir together until mixed thoroughly. Leave to cool.

3 Shape the mixture into 4 oval potato patties, about 1 in. thick. Dip first in the beaten egg, allowing the excess to fall back into the bowl, then coat in the polenta. Refrigerate for at least 30 minutes.

4 Meanwhile, mix together all the ingredients for the salsa. Spoon into a serving bowl, cover with plastic wrap, and leave at room temperature to allow the flavors to develop.

5 Heat the oil in a skillet and cook the potato patties for 4–5 minutes on each side. Serve with the salsa and salad leaves.

FOOD FACT

Polenta is finely ground, golden cornmeal from Italy. It is often made into a soft, savory mixture of the same name, but also makes an excellent coating for foods, such as these potato cakes.

CHEESE & ONION OAT PIE

INGREDIENTS   Serves 4

4 tsp. sunflower oil

2 tbsp. butter

2 medium onions, peeled and
   sliced

1 garlic clove, peeled and
   crushed

1¾ cups rolled oats

1 cup shredded sharp cheddar
   cheese

2 medium eggs, lightly beaten

2 tbsp. freshly chopped
   parsley

salt and freshly ground black
   pepper

1 baking potato, weighing
   about 10 oz., peeled

1 Preheat the oven to 350° F. Heat the oil and half the butter in a saucepan until melted. Add the onions and garlic, and gently cook for 10 minutes or until soft. Remove from the heat and transfer to a large bowl.

2 Spread the oats out on a baking sheet and toast in the hot oven for 12 minutes. Let cool, then add to the onions with the cheese, eggs, and parsley. Season to taste with salt and pepper, and mix well.

3 Line the base of an 8-in. round cake pan with waxed paper and grease well. Thinly slice the potato and arrange the slices on the base, overlapping them slightly.

4 Spoon the cheese and oat mixture on top of the potato, spreading evenly with the back of a spoon. Cover with foil and bake for 30 minutes.

5 Invert the pie onto a baking sheet so that the potato slices are on top. Carefully remove the pan and lining paper.

6 Set the oven to broil. Melt the remaining butter, and carefully brush over the potato topping. Cook under the broiler for 5–6 minutes, until the potatoes are lightly browned. Cut into wedges and serve.

TASTY TIP

To add extra flavor to this dish, cook the onions very slowly until soft and just beginning to brown and caramelize—either white or red onions can be used. For a crunchier texture, add ½ cup chopped hazelnuts instead of ⅓ cup of the oats, adding them to the baking sheet for the last 5 minutes of cooking time, in step 2.

VEGETABLE & GOAT CHEESE PIZZA

INGREDIENTS   Serves 4

4 oz. baking potato
1 tbsp. olive oil
2 cups white bread flour
½ tsp. salt
1 tsp. active dried yeast

FOR THE TOPPING:
1 medium eggplant, thinly
  sliced
2 small zucchini, trimmed and
  sliced lengthwise
1 yellow bell pepper,
  quartered and deseeded

1 red onion, peeled and sliced
  into very thin wedges
5 tbsp. olive oil
1½ cups halved, cooked new
  potatoes
14-oz. can chopped tomatoes,
  drained
2 tsp. freshly chopped
  oregano
⅓ cup diced mozzarella cheese
⅓ cup diced or crumbled goat
  cheese

1 Preheat the oven to 425° F.
  Put a cookie sheet in the oven
to heat up. Cook the potato in
lightly salted, boiling water until
tender. Peel and mash with the
olive oil until smooth.

2 Sift the flour and salt into a
  bowl. Stir in the yeast. Add
the mashed potato and ⅔ cup
warm water, and mix to a soft
dough. Knead for 5–6 minutes,
until smooth. Put the dough in a
bowl, cover with plastic wrap,
and leave to rise in a warm place
for 30 minutes.

3 To make the topping, arrange
  the eggplant, zucchini,
pepper, and onion, skin-side up,
on a rack and brush with 4
tablespoons of the oil. Broil for
4–5 minutes. Turn the vegetables

and brush with the remaining oil.
Broil for 3–4 minutes. Cool,
skin, and slice the pepper. Put all
of the vegetables in a bowl, add
the halved new potatoes, and toss
gently together. Set aside.

4 Briefly reknead the dough
  then roll out to a 12–14 in.
round, according to preferred
thickness. Mix the tomatoes and
oregano together, and spread over
the pizza base. Sprinkle with the
mozzarella cheese. Put the pizza
on the preheated baking sheet
and bake for 8 minutes.

5 Arrange the vegetables and
  goat cheese on top and bake
for 8–10 minutes. Serve.

Chunky Vegetable & Fennel Goulash with Dumplings

INGREDIENTS   Serves 4

2 fennel bulbs, weighing about
   1 lb.
2 tbsp. sunflower oil
1 large onion, peeled and
   sliced
1½ tbsp. paprika
1 tbsp. all-purpose flour
1¼ cups vegetable stock
14-oz. can chopped tomatoes
2⅔ cups diced, peeled
   potatoes
¼ lb. small button mushrooms
salt and freshly ground black
   pepper

FOR THE DUMPLINGS:
1 tbsp. sunflower oil
1 small onion, peeled and
   finely chopped
1 medium egg
3 tbsp. milk
3 tbsp. freshly chopped
   parsley
2 cups fresh white bread
   crumbs

1 Cut the fennel bulbs in half widthwise. Thickly slice the stalks and cut the bulbs into 8 wedges. Heat the oil in a large saucepan or flameproof casserole. Add the onion and fennel, and cook gently for 10 minutes until soft. Stir in the paprika and flour.

2 Remove from the heat and gradually stir in the stock. Add the chopped tomatoes, potatoes, and mushrooms. Season to taste with salt and pepper. Bring to a boil, reduce the heat, and simmer for 20 minutes.

3 Meanwhile, make the dumplings. Heat the oil in a skillet and gently cook the onion for 10 minutes until soft. Leave to cool for a few minutes.

4 In a bowl, beat the egg and milk together, then add the onion, parsley, and bread crumbs, and season to taste. With damp hands, form the mixture into 12 round dumplings, each about the size of a walnut.

5 Arrange the dumplings on top of the goulash. Cover and cook for an additional 15 minutes until the dumplings are cooked and the vegetables are tender. Serve immediately.

TASTY TIP

Sour cream or crème fraîche is delicious spooned on top of the goulash.

CREAMY VEGETABLE KORMA

INGREDIENTS

Serves 4–6

2 tbsp. ghee or vegetable oil

1 large onion, peeled and chopped

2 garlic cloves, peeled and crushed

1-in. piece of ginger, peeled and grated

4 green cardamom pods

2 tsp. ground coriander

1 tsp. ground cumin

1 tsp. ground turmeric

finely grated zest and juice of ½ lemon

½ cup ground almonds

1¾ cups vegetable stock

2⅔ cups peeled and diced potatoes

1 lb. mixed vegetables, such as cauliflower, carrots, and turnips, cut into chunks

⅔ cup heavy cream

3 tbsp. freshly chopped cilantro

salt and freshly ground black pepper

naan bread, to serve

1 Heat the ghee or oil in a large saucepan. Add the onion and cook for 5 minutes. Stir in the garlic and ginger, and cook for an additional 5 minutes or until soft and just beginning to brown.

2 Stir in the cardamom, coriander, cumin, and turmeric. Continue cooking over a low heat for 1 minute, while stirring.

3 Stir in the lemon zest and juice, and almonds. Blend in the vegetable stock. Slowly bring to a boil, stirring occasionally.

4 Add the potatoes and vegetables. Bring back to a boil, then reduce the heat, cover, and simmer for 35–40 minutes, or until the vegetables are just tender. Check after 25 minutes and add more stock if needed.

5 Slowly stir in the cream and chopped cilantro. Season to taste with salt and pepper. Cook very gently until heated through, but do not boil. Serve immediately with naan bread.

FOOD FACT

Ghee is butter, clarified by gently heating until all the water has evaporated and the milk solids separate from the pure fat, which can be used to cook at high temperatures without burning. You can buy butter-based ghee as well as a vegetable oil version in specialty shops and Indian groceries.

CABBAGE TIMBALE

INGREDIENTS

Serves 4–6

1 small savoy cabbage,
  weighing about ¾ lb.
salt and freshly ground black
  pepper
2 tbsp. olive oil
1 leek, trimmed and chopped
1 garlic clove, peeled and
  crushed
½ cup long-grain rice
7-oz. can chopped tomatoes

1¼ cups vegetable stock
14-oz. can kidney beans,
  drained and rinsed
¾ cup shredded cheddar cheese
1 tbsp. freshly chopped
  oregano

TO GARNISH

plain yogurt with paprika
tomato wedges

1 Preheat the oven to 350° F. Remove 6 of the outer leaves of the cabbage. Cut off the thickest part of the stalk and blanch the leaves in lightly salted, boiling water for 2 minutes. Lift out with a slotted spoon, briefly rinse under cold water, and set aside.

2 Remove the stalks from the rest of the cabbage leaves. Shred the leaves and blanch in the boiling water for 1 minute. Drain, rinse under cold water, and pat dry on paper towels.

3 Heat the oil in a skillet and cook the leek and garlic for 5 minutes. Stir in the rice, chopped tomatoes with their juice, and stock. Bring to a boil, cover, and simmer for 15 minutes.

4 Remove the lid and simmer for an additional 4–5 minutes, stirring frequently, until the liquid is absorbed and the rice is tender. Stir in the kidney beans, cheese, and oregano. Season to taste with salt and pepper.

5 Line a greased, deep bowl with some of the large cabbage leaves, overlapping them slightly. Fill with alternate layers of rice mixture and shredded leaves, pressing down well.

6 Cover the top with the remaining leaves. Cover with greased foil and bake in the preheated oven for 30 minutes. Let stand for 10 minutes. Turn out, cut into wedges, and serve with yogurt, sprinkled with paprika and tomato wedges.

HANDY HINT

Avoid red or white cabbage for this recipe, as their leaves are not flexible enough.

INDONESIAN SALAD WITH PEANUT DRESSING

INGREDIENTS

Serves 4

½ lb. new potatoes, scrubbed
1 large carrot, peeled and
    thinly sliced
¾ cup trimmed green beans
½ lb. tiny cauliflower florets
¾ cup cucumber, thinly sliced
1½ cups fresh bean sprouts
3 medium eggs, hard-boiled
    and quartered

FOR THE PEANUT DRESSING:

2 tbsp. sesame oil
1 garlic clove, peeled and
    crushed
1 red chili, deseeded and
    finely chopped
⅔ cup crunchy peanut butter
6 tbsp. hot vegetable stock
2 tsp. light brown sugar
2 tsp. dark soy sauce
1 tbsp. lime juice

1 Cook the potatoes in a saucepan of salted, boiling water for 15–20 minutes until tender. Remove with a slotted spoon and slice thickly into a large bowl. Keep the saucepan of water boiling.

2 Add the carrot, green beans, and cauliflower to the water, return to a boil, and cook for 2 minutes or until just tender. Drain and rinse under cold running water, then drain well. Add to the potatoes with the cucumber and bean sprouts.

3 To make the dressing, gently heat the sesame oil in a small saucepan. Add the garlic and chili and cook for a few seconds, then remove from the heat. Stir in the peanut butter.

4 Stir in the stock, a little at a time. Add the remaining ingredients and mix together to make a thick, creamy dressing.

5 Divide the vegetables between 4 plates and arrange the eggs on top. Drizzle the dressing over the salad and serve immediately.

HELPFUL HINT

For perfect hard-boiled eggs with no green rings around the yolks, put the eggs in a saucepan and bring to a boil. Cover and remove from the heat. Allow eggs to sit for 15 minutes. Plunge in cold water, then refrigerate.

LAYERED CHEESE & HERB POTATO CAKE

INGREDIENTS   Serves 4

2 lbs. waxy potatoes
3 tbsp. freshly cut chives
2 tbsp. freshly chopped
    parsley
2 cups shredded mature
    cheddar cheese
2 large egg yolks
1 tsp. paprika
2 cups fresh white bread
    crumbs

½ cup toasted and roughly
    chopped almonds
¼ cup butter, melted
salt and freshly ground black
    pepper
mixed salad or steamed
    vegetables, to serve

1 Preheat the oven to 350° F. Lightly grease and line the base of an 8-in. round cake pan with lightly greased waxed paper. Peel and thinly slice the potatoes and set aside. Stir the chives, parsley, cheese, and egg yolks together in a small bowl and set aside. Mix the paprika into the bread crumbs.

2 Sprinkle the almonds over the base of the lined pan. Cover with half the potatoes, arranging them in layers, then sprinkle with the paprika and bread-crumb mixture, and season to taste with salt and pepper.

3 Spoon the cheese and herb mixture over the bread crumbs, sprinkle with a little more seasoning, then arrange the remaining potatoes on top. Drizzle the melted butter over and press the surface down firmly.

4 Bake in the preheated oven for 1¼ hours or until golden and cooked through. Let the potato cake stand for 10 minutes before carefully turning out and serving in thick wedges. Serve immediately with salad or freshly cooked vegetables.

HANDY HINT

Check that the potatoes are tender all the way through by pushing a thin skewer through the center. If the potatoes are still a little hard, and the top is already brown enough, loosely cover with aluminum foil and continue cooking until done.

ROAST BABY POTATO SALAD

INGREDIENTS   Serves 4

¾ lb. small shallots
sea salt and freshly ground
   black pepper
2 lbs. small, even-sized new
   potatoes
2 tbsp. olive oil
2 medium zucchini

2 sprigs of fresh rosemary
½ lb. cherry tomatoes
⅔ cup sour cream
2 tbsp. freshly cut chives
¼ tsp. paprika

1 Preheat the oven to 400° F. Trim the shallots, but leave the skins on. Put in a saucepan of lightly salted, boiling water with the potatoes, and cook for 5 minutes; drain. Separate the shallots and plunge them into cold water for 1 minute.

2 Put the oil on a baking sheet lined with aluminum foil or a roasting pan, and heat for a few minutes. Peel the skins off the shallots—they should now come away easily. Add to the baking sheet or roasting pan with the potatoes, and toss in the oil to coat. Sprinkle with a little sea salt. Roast in the preheated oven for 10 minutes.

3 Meanwhile, trim the zucchini, halve them lengthwise, and cut them into 2-in. chunks. Add to the baking sheet or roasting pan, toss to mix, and cook for 5 minutes.

4 Pierce the tomato skins with a sharp knife. Add to the sheet or pan with the rosemary, and cook for an additional 5 minutes or until all the vegetables are tender. Remove the rosemary and discard. Grind a little black pepper over the vegetables.

5 Spoon into a wide serving bowl. Mix together the sour cream and chives, and drizzle over the vegetables just before serving.

TASTY TIP

For a more substantial salad, or to serve six people rather than four, add ½ lb. eggplant, cut it in half lengthwise, and cook with the potatoes and shallots, along with an extra 1 tablespoon olive oil. If desired, crème fraîche or plain yogurt may be used instead of the sour cream.

RICE NUGGETS IN HERBED TOMATO SAUCE

INGREDIENTS   Serves 4

2½ cups vegetable stock
1 bay leaf
1 cup Arborio rice
½ cup shredded cheddar
  cheese
1 medium egg yolk
1 tbsp. all-purpose flour
2 tbsp. freshly chopped parsley
salt and freshly ground black
  pepper
grated Parmesan cheese, to
  serve

**FOR THE HERBED TOMATO
SAUCE:**
1 tbsp. olive oil
1 onion, peeled and thinly
  sliced
1 garlic clove, peeled and
  crushed
1 small yellow bell pepper,
  deseeded and diced
14-oz. can chopped tomatoes
1 tbsp. freshly chopped basil

1 Pour the stock into a large saucepan. Add the bay leaf. Bring to a boil, add the rice, stir, then cover and simmer for 15 minutes.

2 Uncover, reduce the heat to low, and cook for an additional 5 minutes until the rice is tender and all the stock is absorbed, stirring often. Cool.

3 Stir the cheese, egg yolk, flour, and parsley into the rice. Season to taste, then shape into 20 walnut-sized balls. Cover and refrigerate.

4 To make the sauce, heat the oil in a large skillet and cook the onion for 5 minutes. Add the garlic and bell pepper, and cook for an additional 5 minutes until soft.

5 Stir in the chopped tomatoes and simmer gently for 3 minutes. Stir in the chopped basil and season to taste.

6 Add the rice nuggets to the sauce and simmer for an additional 10 minutes or until the rice nuggets are cooked through and the sauce has reduced a little. Spoon onto serving plates and serve hot, sprinkled with Parmesan cheese.

HELPFUL HINT

It is important that the stock is absorbed completely by the rice if these nuggets are to hold their shape. Stir constantly for the last minute of cooking to prevent the rice from sticking or burning.

MIXED GRAIN PILAF

INGREDIENTS

Serves 4

2 tbsp. olive oil
1 garlic clove, peeled and
  crushed
½ tsp. ground turmeric
⅔ cup mixed long-grain and
  wild rice
heaping ⅓ cup red lentils
1¼ cups vegetable stock
7-oz. can chopped tomatoes
2-in. piece cinnamon stick

salt and freshly ground black
  pepper
14-oz. can mixed beans,
  drained and rinsed
1 tbsp. butter
1 bunch scallions, trimmed
  and finely sliced
3 medium eggs
4 tbsp. freshly chopped herbs,
  such as parsley and chervil
sprigs of fresh dill, to garnish

1 Heat 1 tablespoon of the oil in a saucepan. Add the garlic and turmeric, and cook for a few seconds. Stir in the rice and lentils.

2 Add the stock, tomatoes, and cinnamon. Season to taste with salt and pepper. Stir once and bring to a boil. Lower the heat, cover, and simmer for 20 minutes until most of the stock is absorbed and the rice and lentils are tender.

3 Stir in the beans, replace the lid, and let stand for 2–3 minutes to allow the beans to heat through.

4 While the rice is cooking, heat the remaining oil and butter in a skillet. Add the scallions and cook for 4–5 minutes until soft. Lightly beat the eggs with 2 tablespoons of the herbs, then season with salt and pepper.

5 Pour the egg mixture over the scallions. Stir gently with a spatula over a low heat, drawing the mixture from the sides to the center as the omelette sets. When almost set, stop stirring, and cook for about 30 seconds, until golden underneath.

6 Remove the omelette from the pan, roll up, and slice into thin strips. Fluff up the rice with a fork and remove the cinnamon stick. Spoon onto serving plates, and top with strips of omelette and the remaining chopped herbs. Garnish with dill and serve.

HELPFUL HINT

Long-grain rice and wild rice have different cooking times, but in ready-mixed packages, the rice has been treated to even out the cooking times, making preparation easier.

Calypso Rice with Curried Bananas

INGREDIENTS   Serves 4

2 tbsp. sunflower oil
1 medium onion, peeled and
  finely chopped
1 garlic clove, peeled and
  crushed
1 red chili, deseeded and
  finely chopped
1 red bell pepper, deseeded
  and chopped
1⅓ cups basmati rice
juice of 1 lime
1½ cups vegetable stock

7-oz. can black-eyed peas,
  drained and rinsed
2 tbsp. freshly chopped parsley
salt and freshly ground black
  pepper
sprigs of cilantro, to garnish

FOR THE CURRIED BANANAS:
4 green bananas
2 tbsp. sunflower oil
2 tsp. mild curry paste
¾ cup coconut milk

1 Heat the oil in a large skillet and gently cook the onion for 10 minutes until soft. Add the garlic, chili, and red pepper, and cook for 2–3 minutes.

2 Rinse the rice under cold running water, then add to the pan and stir. Pour in the lime juice and stock, bring to a boil, cover, and simmer for 12–15 minutes or until the rice is tender and the stock is absorbed.

3 Stir in the black-eyed peas and chopped parsley, and season to taste with salt and pepper. Let stand covered for 5 minutes before serving to allow the beans to warm through.

4 While the rice is cooking, make the curried green bananas. Remove the skins from the bananas—you may have to cut them off with a sharp knife. Slice the flesh thickly. Heat the oil in a skillet and cook the bananas, in 2 batches, for 2–3 minutes or until lightly browned.

5 Pour the coconut milk into the pan, and stir in the curry paste.

6 Add the banana slices to the coconut milk and simmer uncovered over a low heat for 8–10 minutes or until the bananas are very soft and the coconut milk slightly reduced.

7 Spoon the rice onto warmed serving plates, garnish with sprigs of cilantro, and serve immediately with the curried bananas.

RED LENTIL KEDGEREE WITH AVOCADO & TOMATOES

INGREDIENTS   Serves 4

heaping ¾ cup basmati rice

¾ cup red lentils

½ tbsp. butter

1 tbsp. sunflower oil

1 medium onion, peeled and chopped

1 tsp. ground cumin

4 green cardamom pods, bruised

1 bay leaf

2 cups vegetable or chicken stock

1 ripe avocado, peeled, pitted, and diced

1 tbsp. lemon juice

4 plum tomatoes, peeled and diced

2 tbsp. freshly chopped cilantro

salt and freshly ground black pepper

lemon or lime slices, to garnish

1 Put the rice and lentils in a sieve and rinse under cold running water. Tip into a bowl, then pour over enough cold water to cover, and let soak for 10 minutes.

2 Heat the butter and oil in a saucepan. Add the sliced onion and cook gently, stirring occasionally for 10 minutes until softened. Stir in the cumin, cardamom pods, and bay leaf, and cook for an additional minute, stirring all the time.

3 Drain the rice and lentils, rinse again, and add to the onions in the saucepan. Stir in the vegetable stock and bring to a boil. Reduce the heat, cover the saucepan, and simmer for 15 minutes or until the rice and lentils are tender.

4 Place the diced avocado in a bowl and toss with the lemon juice. Stir in the tomatoes and chopped cilantro. Season to taste with salt and pepper.

5 Fluff up the rice with a fork, spoon into a warmed serving dish, and spoon the avocado mixture on top. Garnish with lemon or lime slices and serve.

TASTY TIP

Although basmati rice and red lentils do not usually need to be presoaked, it improves the results in this recipe: the rice will have very light, fluffy, separate grains, and the lentils will just begin to break down, giving the dish a creamier texture.

ADZUKI BEAN & RICE PATTIES

INGREDIENTS   Serves 4

2½ tbsp. sunflower oil
1 medium onion, peeled and
   very finely chopped
1 garlic clove, peeled and
   crushed
1 tsp. curry paste
1⅛ cups basmati rice
14-oz. can adzuki beans,
   drained and rinsed (kidney
   beans may also be used)
1 cup vegetable stock
¼ lb. firm tofu, crumbled
1 tsp. garam masala
2 tbsp. freshly chopped

cilantro
salt and freshly ground black
   pepper

FOR THE CARROT RAITA:
2 large carrots, peeled and
   shredded
½ cucumber, diced
⅔ cup plain yogurt

TO SERVE:
whole-wheat hamburger buns
tomato slices
lettuce leaves

1 Heat 1 tablespoon of the oil in a saucepan and gently cook the onion for 10 minutes until soft. Add the garlic and curry paste, and cook for a few more seconds. Stir in the rice and beans.

2 Pour in the stock, bring to a boil, and simmer for 12 minutes or until all the stock has been absorbed—do not lift the lid for the first 10 minutes of cooking. Set aside.

3 Lightly mash the tofu. Add to the rice mixture with the garam masala, cilantro, salt, and pepper. Mix.

4 Shape the mixture in 8 patties. Chill in the refrigerator for 30 minutes.

5 Meanwhile, make the raita. Mix together the carrots, cucumber, and plain yogurt. Spoon into a small bowl and chill in the refrigerator until ready to serve.

6 Heat the remaining oil in a large skillet. Fry the patties, in batches if necessary, for 4–5 minutes on each side or until lightly browned. Serve in the buns with tomato slices and lettuce. Accompany with the raita.

FOOD FACT

Firm tofu is sold in blocks. It is made in a similar way to soft cheese, and is the pressed curds of soy milk.

WILD RICE DOLMADES

INGREDIENTS   Serves 4–6

6 tbsp. olive oil
2½ tbsp. pine nuts
1½ cups wiped and finely
   chopped mushrooms
4 scallions, trimmed and finely
   chopped
1 garlic clove, peeled and
   crushed
1 cup cooked wild rice
2 tsp. freshly chopped dill
2 tsp. freshly chopped mint

salt and freshly ground black
   pepper
16–24 prepared medium grape
   leaves
about 1¼ cups vegetable stock

TO GARNISH:
lemon wedges
sprigs of fresh dill

1 Heat 1 tbsp. of the oil in a
skillet and gently cook the
pine nuts for 2–3 minutes,
stirring frequently, until golden.
Remove from the pan and set
aside.

2 Add 1½ tablespoons of oil to
the pan and gently cook the
mushrooms, scallions, and garlic
for 7–8 minutes until very soft.
Stir in the rice, herbs, salt, and
pepper.

3 Put a heaping teaspoon of
stuffing in the center of each
leaf (if the leaves are small, put 2
together, overlapping slightly).
Fold over the stalk end, then the
sides, and roll up to make a neat
pocket. Continue until all the
stuffing is used.

4 Arrange the stuffed grape
leaves close together, seam-
side down, in a large saucepan,
drizzling each with a little of the

remaining oil—there will be
several layers. Pour over just
enough stock to cover.

5 Put an inverted plate over the
dolmades to keep them from
unrolling during cooking. Bring
to a boil, then simmer very gently
for 3 minutes. Cool in the
saucepan.

6 Transfer the dolmades to a
serving dish. Cover and chill.
Sprinkle with pine nuts, and
garnish with lemon and dill.

HELPFUL HINT

Fresh grape leaves should be
blanched for 2–3 minutes in
boiling water. Grape leaves
preserved in brine can be
found in supermarkets—soak
in warm water for 20 minutes
before using.

Fava Bean & Artichoke Risotto

INGREDIENTS   Serves 4

2½ cups frozen fava beans

14-oz. can artichoke hearts, drained

1 tbsp. sunflower oil

⅔ cup dry white wine

3¾ cups vegetable stock

2 tbsp. butter

1 onion, peeled and finely chopped

heaping 1 cup Arborio rice

zest and juice of 1 lemon

½ cup grated Parmesan cheese

salt and freshly ground black pepper

freshly grated Parmesan cheese, to serve

1 Cook the beans in a saucepan of lightly salted, boiling water for 4–5 minutes or until just tender. Drain and plunge into cold water. Peel off the tough outer skins, if desired. Pat the artichokes dry on paper towels and cut each in half lengthwise through the stem end. Cut each half into 3 wedges.

2 Heat the oil in a large saucepan and cook the artichokes for 4–5 minutes, turning occasionally, until they are lightly browned. Remove and set aside. Bring the wine and stock to a boil in a separate pan. Keep them barely simmering.

3 Melt the butter in a large skillet, add the onion, and cook for 5 minutes until beginning to soften. Add the rice and cook for 1 minute, stirring.

Pour in a ladleful of the hot wine and stock, simmer gently, stirring frequently, until the stock is absorbed. Continue to add the stock in this way for 20–25 minutes until the rice is just tender; the risotto should look creamy and soft.

4 Add the fava beans, artichokes, and lemon zest and juice. Gently mix in, cover, and leave to warm through for 1–2 minutes. Stir in the Parmesan cheese, and season to taste with salt and pepper. Serve sprinkled with extra Parmesan cheese.

HELPFUL HINT

If using fresh fava beans, buy about 1½ lb. in their pods. Young fresh beans do not need to be skinned.

MEDITERRANEAN RICE SALAD

INGREDIENTS

Serves 4

1½ cups Camargue red rice

2 sun-dried tomatoes, finely chopped

2 garlic cloves, peeled and finely chopped

4 tbsp. oil from a jar of sun-dried tomatoes

2 tsp. balsamic vinegar

2 tsp. red wine vinegar

salt and freshly ground black pepper

1 red onion, peeled and thinly sliced

1 yellow bell pepper, quartered and deseeded

1 red bell pepper, quartered and deseeded

½ cucumber, peeled and diced

6 ripe plum tomatoes, cut into wedges

1 fennel bulb, halved and thinly sliced

fresh basil leaves, to garnish

1 Cook the rice in a saucepan of lightly salted, boiling water for 35–40 minutes or until tender. Drain well and set aside.

2 Whisk the sun-dried tomatoes, garlic, oil, and vinegars together in a small bowl or pitcher. Season to taste with salt and pepper. Put the red onion in a large bowl, pour over the dressing, and leave to allow the flavors to develop.

3 Put the peppers skin-side up on a rack, and cook under a broiler for 5–6 minutes or until charred. Remove and place in a plastic bag. When cool enough to handle, peel off the skins and slice the peppers.

4 Add the peppers, cucumber, tomatoes, fennel, and rice to the onions. Mix gently together to coat in the dressing. Cover and chill in the refrigerator for 30 minutes to allow the flavors to mingle.

5 Remove the salad from the refrigerator and let stand at room temperature for 20 minutes. Garnish with fresh basil leaves and serve.

FOOD FACT

Camargue red rice from the south of France is a reddish-brown color and gives salad a stunning appearance. It has a texture and cooking time similar to that of brown rice, which may be substituted in this recipe if Camargue red rice is unavailable.

CHEF'S RICE SALAD

INGREDIENTS

Serves 4

1⅓ cups wild rice
½ cucumber
½ lb. cherry tomatoes
6 scallions, trimmed
5 tbsp. extra-virgin olive oil
2 tbsp. balsamic vinegar
1 tsp. Dijon mustard
1 tsp. superfine sugar
salt and freshly ground black
  pepper
1 cup arugula

¼ lb. bacon
½ cup finely diced, cooked
  chicken meat
1 cup shredded Emmentaler
  cheese
¾ cup large cooked shrimp,
  peeled
1 avocado, pitted, peeled, and
  sliced, to garnish
warm, crusty bread, to serve

1 Put the rice in a saucepan of water and bring to a boil, stirring once or twice. Reduce the heat, cover, and simmer gently for 30–50 minutes, depending on the texture desired. Drain well and set aside.

2 Thinly peel the cucumber, cut in half, then remove the seeds with a spoon. Cut the cucumber into thin slices. Cut the tomatoes in quarters. Cut the scallions into diagonal slices.

3 Whisk the olive oil with the vinegar, then whisk in the Dijon mustard and sugar. Season the dressing with salt and pepper.

4 In a large bowl, gently toss together the cooled rice with the tomatoes, cucumber, scallions, and arugula. Pour over the dressing and toss lightly together.

5 Grill the bacon on both sides for 4–6 minutes or until crisp. Remove and chop. Arrange the prepared arugula salad on a platter, then arrange the bacon, chicken, cheese, and shrimp on top. Garnish with avocado slices, and serve with plenty of warm, crusty bread.

TASTY TIP

You can use any combination of your favorite cold meats in this salad; smoked duck or chicken work particularly well. Emmentaler cheese, famous for its large, round holes, has a mellow and sweet flavor that is good in this salad, or you can use your favorite hard cheese, such as cheddar or edam.

RICE WITH SMOKED SALMON & GINGER

INGREDIENTS   Serves 4

1⅓ cups basmati rice
2½ cups fish stock
1 bunch scallions, trimmed
  and diagonally sliced
3 tbsp. freshly chopped
  cilantro
1 tsp. freshly grated root
  ginger

½ lb. sliced smoked salmon
2 tbsp. soy sauce
1 tsp. sesame oil
2 tsp. lemon juice
4–6 slices pickled ginger
2 tsp. sesame seeds
arugula leaves, to serve

1 Place the rice in a sieve and rinse under cold water until the water runs clear. Drain, then place in a large saucepan with the stock and bring gently to a boil. Reduce to a simmer and cover with an airtight lid. Cook for 10 minutes, then remove from the heat and let sit, covered, for an additional 10 minutes.

2 Stir the scallions, cilantro, and fresh ginger into the cooked rice and mix well.

3 Spoon the rice into 4 tart pans, each measuring 4 in., and press down firmly with the back of a spoon to form patties. Invert a pan onto an individual serving plate, then tap the base firmly, and remove the pan. Repeat with the rest of the pans.

4 Top the rice with the salmon, folding if necessary, so the sides of the rice can still be seen in places. Mix together the soy sauce, sesame oil, and lemon juice to make a dressing, then drizzle over the salmon. Top with the pickled ginger and a sprinkling of sesame seeds. Scatter the arugula leaves around the edge of the plates, and serve immediately.

FOOD FACT

Good smoked salmon should look moist and firm, and have a peachy pink color. If you buy it from a delicatessan counter, ask for it to be freshly sliced, as any that has already been sliced may be dried out. Vacuum-packed salmon will keep for about 2 weeks in the refrigerator (check the use-by date), but once opened should be used within 3 days.

SWEET & SOUR RICE WITH CHICKEN

INGREDIENTS   Serves 4

4 scallions

2 tsp. sesame oil

1 tsp. Chinese five-spice powder

1 lb. chicken breast, cut into cubes

1 tbsp. oil

1 garlic clove, peeled and crushed

1 medium onion, peeled and sliced into thin wedges

1⅓ cups long-grain white rice

2½ cups water

4 tbsp. ketchup

1 tbsp. tomato paste

2 tbsp. honey

1 tbsp. vinegar

1 tbsp. dark soy sauce

1 carrot, peeled and thinly sliced

1 Trim the scallions, then cut lengthwise into fine strips. Drop into a large bowl of ice water and set aside.

2 Mix together the sesame oil and Chinese five-spice powder, and use to rub into the cubed chicken. Heat the wok, then add the oil, and when hot, cook the garlic and onion for 2–3 minutes or until transparent and softened.

3 Add the chicken and stir-fry over a medium-high heat until the chicken is golden and cooked through. Using a slotted spoon, remove from the wok and keep warm.

4 Stir the rice into the wok and add the water, ketchup, tomato paste, honey, vinegar, and soy sauce. Stir well to mix. Bring

to a boil, then simmer until almost all of the liquid is absorbed. Stir in the carrots and chicken, and continue to cook for 3–4 minutes.

5 Drain the scallions, which will have become curly. Garnish with the scallion curls, and serve immediately with the rice and chicken.

FOOD FACT

Five-spice powder is a popular Chinese seasoning available in most supermarkets. It is a mixture of finely ground star anise, fennel, cinnamon, cloves, and Szechuan pepper, and adds a unique sweet and spicy aniseed flavor to food.

SALMON & PHYLLO POCKETS

INGREDIENTS   Serves 4

1 tbsp. sunflower or vegetable oil
1 bunch of scallions, trimmed and finely chopped
1 tsp. paprika
1 cup long-grain white rice
1¼ cups fish stock
salt and freshly ground black pepper

1 lb. salmon fillet, cubed
1 tbsp. freshly chopped parsley
zest and juice of 1 lemon
1¼ cups arugula
generous ¼ lb. spinach
12 sheets phyllo pastry
¼ cup butter, melted

1 Preheat the oven to 400° F. Heat the oil in a small frying pan and gently cook the scallions for 2 minutes. Stir in the paprika and continue to cook for 1 minute, then remove from the heat and set aside.

2 Put the rice in a sieve and rinse under cold running water until the water runs clear; drain. Put the rice and stock in a saucepan, bring to a boil, then cover and simmer for 10 minutes or until the liquid is absorbed and the rice is tender. Add the scallion mixture and fork through. Season to taste with salt and pepper, then let cool.

3 In a nonmetallic bowl, mix together the salmon, parsley, lemon zest and juice, and salt and pepper. Set aside.

4 Blanch the arugula and spinach in a large saucepan of boiling water for 30 seconds or until just wilted. Drain well in a colander, and rinse in plenty of cold water, then squeeze out as much moisture as possible.

5 Brush 3 sheets of phyllo pastry with melted butter and lay them on top of one another. Take a quarter of the rice mixture, and arrange it in an oblong shape in the center of the pastry. On top of this place a quarter of the salmon, followed by a quarter of the arugula and spinach.

6 Draw up the pastry around the filling and twist at the top to create a pocket. Repeat with the remaining pastry and filling to make 4 pockets. Brush with the remaining butter.

7 Place the pockets on a lightly greased baking sheet, and cook in the preheated oven for 20 minutes or until golden brown. Serve immediately.

WILD MUSHROOM RISOTTO

INGREDIENTS   Serves 4

½ oz. dried porcini

5 cups vegetable or chicken stock

⅓ cup butter

1 tbsp. olive oil

1 onion, peeled and chopped

2–4 garlic cloves, peeled and chopped

1–2 red chilies, deseeded and chopped

½ lb. wild mushrooms, halved if large

¼ lb. button mushrooms, wiped and sliced

2 cups Arborio rice

1 cup large cooked shrimp, peeled

⅔ cup white wine

salt and freshly ground black pepper

1 tbsp. lemon zest

1 tbsp. freshly cut chives

2 tbsp. freshly chopped parsley

1 Soak the porcini in 1¼ cups of very hot, but not boiling water for 30 minutes. Drain, setting aside the mushrooms and soaking liquid. Pour the stock into a saucepan, and bring to a boil, then reduce the heat to keep it simmering.

2 Melt the butter and oil in a large, deep skillet, add the onion, garlic, and chilies, and cook gently for 5 minutes. Add the mushrooms, along with the drained porcini, and continue to cook for 4–5 minutes, stirring frequently.

3 Stir in the rice and cook for 1 minute. Strain the soaking liquid and stir into the rice with a little of the hot stock. Cook gently, stirring frequently, until the liquid is absorbed. Continue to add most of the stock, a ladleful at a time, cooking after

each addition, until the rice is tender and the risotto looks creamy.

4 Add the shrimp and wine along with the last additions of stock. When the shrimp are hot and all the liquid is absorbed, season with salt and pepper. Remove from the heat and stir in the lemon zest, chives, and parsley, setting aside some for the garnish. Garnish and serve.

FOOD FACT

Porcini are wild mushrooms, also known by their French name *cèpes*. They have a meaty texture and an almost woody taste. Dried porcini are expensive, but you only need the tiniest amount to add an incredibly intense mushroom flavor to this risotto.

SPECIAL FRIED RICE

INGREDIENTS

Serves 4

1 large egg
1 tsp. sesame oil
1⅓ cups long-grain white rice
1 tbsp. peanut oil
1 lb. boneless, skinless
  chicken breast, diced
8 scallions, trimmed and
  sliced
2 large carrots, trimmed and
  thinly sliced
¾ cup snow peas

¾ cup raw tiger shrimp, peeled
2 tsp. Chinese five-spice
  powder
1 tbsp. soy sauce
1 tbsp. Thai fish sauce
1 tbsp. rice wine vinegar

1 Beat the egg in a bowl with ½ teaspoon of the sesame oil and 2 teaspoons of water. Heat a skillet over a medium-high heat, and swirl in 2 tablespoons of the egg mixture to form a paper-thin omelette. Remove and set aside. Repeat this process until all the egg has been used.

2 Cook the rice in lightly salted, boiling water for 12 minutes or until tender. Drain and set aside.

3 Heat a wok, then add the remaining sesame oil with the peanut oil, and stir-fry the chicken for 5 minutes until cooked through. Using a slotted spoon, remove from the wok and keep warm.

4 Add the scallions, carrot, and snow peas to the wok, and stir-fry for 2–3 minutes. Add the shrimp and stir-fry for 2–3

minutes, or until pink. Return the chicken to the wok with the Chinese five-spice powder, and stir-fry for 1 minute. Stir in the drained rice.

5 Mix together the soy sauce, fish sauce, and vinegar. Pour into the wok and continue to stir-fry for 2–3 minutes. Roll the papery omelettes into tight rolls and slice to form thin strips. Stir into the rice and serve immediately.

FOOD FACT

A classic Chinese ingredient, sesame oil is richly colored and strongly flavored. It has a low smoking temperature, so should not be heated to an extremely high temperature, otherwise the delicious sesame flavor will be lost.

LEG OF LAMB WITH MINTED RICE

INGREDIENTS   Serves 4

1 tbsp. olive oil

1 medium onion, peeled and finely chopped

1 garlic clove, peeled and crushed

1 celery stalk, trimmed and chopped

1 large mild red chili, deseeded and chopped

½ cup long-grain rice

⅔ cup lamb or chicken stock

2 tbsp. freshly chopped mint

salt and freshly ground black pepper

3 lb. boned leg of lamb

freshly cooked vegetables, to serve

1 Preheat the oven to 375° F. Heat the oil in a skillet and gently cook the onion for 5 minutes. Stir in the garlic, celery, and chili, and continue to cook for 3–4 minutes.

2 Place the rice and the stock in a large saucepan, and cook covered for 10–12 minutes or until the rice is tender and all the liquid is absorbed. Stir in the onion and celery mixture, then leave to cool. Once the rice mixture is cold, stir in the chopped mint, and season to taste with salt and pepper.

3 Place the boned lamb skin-side down and spoon the rice mixture along the center of the meat. Roll up the meat to enclose the stuffing and tie securely with string. Place in a roasting pan and roast in the preheated oven for 80 minutes. Remove from the oven and let rest in a warm place for 20 minutes before carving. Serve with a selection of cooked vegetables.

HELPFUL HINT

Weigh the lamb after stuffing and allow it to come to room temperature before roasting. For medium-cooked lamb, allow 25 minutes per pound, plus 25 minutes; for well-done, allow 30 minutes per pound, plus 30 minutes. Use a meat thermometer to check the joint, if cooked, or push a fine skewer into the thickest part: for medium meat they will be pink, for well-done, the juices will run clear.

LEMON CHICKEN RICE

INGREDIENTS

Serves 4

2 tbsp. sunflower or
  vegetable oil
4 chicken leg portions
1 medium onion, peeled and
  chopped
1–2 garlic cloves, peeled and
  crushed
1 tbsp. curry powder
2 tbsp. butter
1⅓ cups long-grain white rice

1 lemon, preferably unwaxed,
  sliced
2½ cups chicken stock
salt and freshly ground black
  pepper
2 tbsp. flaked, toasted
  almonds
sprigs of fresh cilantro, to
  garnish

1 Preheat the oven to 350° F. Heat the oil in a large skillet, add the chicken legs, and cook, turning, until sealed and golden all over. Using a slotted spoon, remove from the pan and set aside.

2 Add the onion and garlic to the oil remaining in the frying pan, and cook for 5–7 minutes, or until just beginning to brown. Sprinkle in the curry powder and cook, stirring, for an additional 1 minute. Return the chicken to the pan and stir well, then remove from the heat.

3 Melt the butter in a large heavy-based saucepan. Add the rice and cook, stirring, to ensure that all the grains are coated in the melted butter, then remove from the heat.

4 Stir the lemon slices into the chicken mixture, then spoon the mixture onto the rice, and pour over the stock. Season to taste with salt and pepper.

5 Cover with an airtight lid and cook in the preheated oven for 45 minutes or until the rice is tender and the chicken is cooked thoroughly. Serve sprinkled with the toasted flaked almonds, and sprigs of cilantro.

TASTY TIP

Choose a strength of curry powder according to personal taste. There is a huge range of brands and mixtures available, from mild korma to medium Madras or hot vindaloo. Unless you use spices frequently, buy them in small quantities, as they quickly become stale and lose their flavor. Store in glass jars in a cool, dark place.

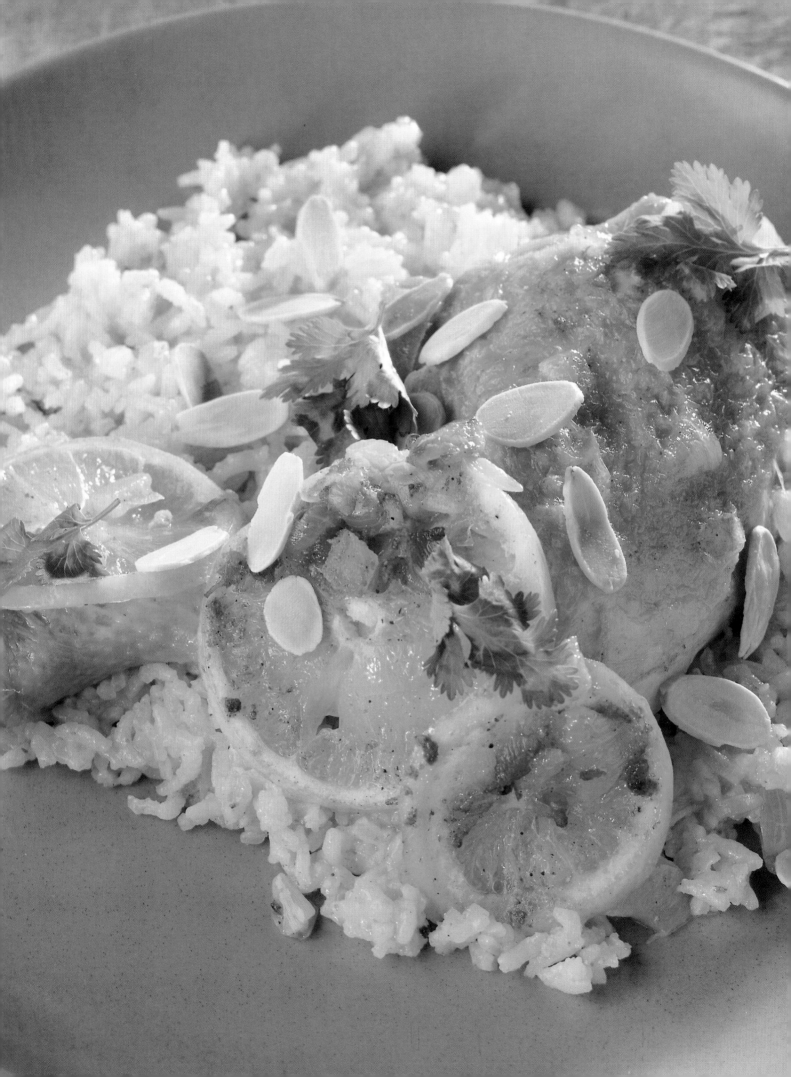

SCALLOP & POTATO GRATIN

INGREDIENTS   Serves 4

8 fresh scallops
scallop shells, for presentation
4 tbsp. white wine
salt and freshly ground black
  pepper
¼ cup butter
3 tbsp. all-purpose flour

2 tbsp. light cream
½ cup shredded cheddar
  cheese
2⅔ cups peeled and coarsely
  diced potatoes
1 tbsp. milk

1 Preheat the oven to 425° F. Clean 4 scallop shells to use as serving dishes and set aside. Place the scallops in a small saucepan with the wine, ⅔ cup water, and salt and pepper. Cover, and simmer very gently for 5 minutes or until just tender. Remove with a slotted spoon and cut each scallop into 3 pieces. Set aside the cooking juices.

2 Melt half the butter in a saucepan, stir in the flour, and cook for 1 minute, stirring, then gradually whisk in the cooking juices. Simmer, stirring, for 3–4 minutes until the sauce has thickened. Season to taste with salt and pepper. Remove from the heat and stir in the cream and half of the cheese. Fold in the scallops.

3 Boil the potatoes in lightly salted water until tender, then mash with the remaining butter and milk. Spoon or pipe the mashed potatoes around the edges of the cleaned scallop shells.

4 Divide the scallop mixture among the 4 shells, placing the mixture neatly in the center. Sprinkle with the remaining cheese, and bake in the preheated oven for about 10–15 minutes until golden brown and bubbling. Serve immediately.

FOOD FACT

Because scallops perish quickly out of water, they are usually sold shucked. Scallop shells are sold at many fish counters and gourmet stores for serving purposes.

WARM POTATO, PEAR, & PECAN SALAD

INGREDIENTS   Serves 4

2 lbs. new potatoes, preferably
   red-skinned, unpeeled
salt and freshly ground black
   pepper
1 tsp. Dijon mustard
2 tsp. white wine vinegar
3 tbsp. peanut oil

1 tbsp. hazelnut or walnut oil
2 tsp. poppy seeds
2 firm ripe dessert pears
2 tsp. lemon juice
scant ½ lb. baby spinach
   leaves
¾ cup toasted pecans

1 Scrub the potatoes, then cook in a saucepan of lightly salted, boiling water for 15 minutes or until tender. Drain, cut into halves, or quarters if large, and place in a serving bowl.

2 In a small bowl or pitcher, whisk together the mustard and vinegar. Gradually add the oils until the mixture begins to thicken. Stir in the poppy seeds, and season to taste.

3 Pour about two thirds of the dressing over the hot potatoes and toss gently to coat. Leave until the potatoes have soaked up the dressing and are just warm.

4 Meanwhile, quarter and core the pears. Cut into thin slices, then sprinkle with the lemon juice to prevent them from turning brown. Add to the potatoes with the spinach leaves and toasted pecans. Gently mix together.

5 Drizzle the remaining dressing over the salad. Serve immediately before the spinach starts to wilt.

FOOD FACT

To toast the pecans, place on a cookie sheet in a single layer and cook in a preheated oven at 350° F for 5 minutes, or under a broiler for 3–4 minutes, turning frequently. Watch them carefully—they burn easily. If you cannot get red-skinned new potatoes for this dish, add color by using red-skinned pears instead. Look for Red Bartlett, Red Williams, and Napolian.

HERBED HASSELBACK POTATOES WITH ROAST CHICKEN

INGREDIENTS   Serves 4

8 medium, evenly-sized
   potatoes, peeled
3 large sprigs of fresh rosemary
1 tbsp. oil
salt and freshly ground black
   pepper
¾ lb. baby parsnips, peeled
¾ lb. baby carrots, peeled

¾ lb. baby leeks, trimmed
⅓ cup butter
finely grated zest of 1 lemon,
   preferably unwaxed
3½ lbs. chicken

1 Preheat the oven to 400° F.
Place a chopstick on either
side of a potato, and with a sharp
knife, cut down through the
potato until you reach the
chopsticks; take care not to cut
right through the potato. Repeat
these cuts every ¼ in. along the
length of the potato. Carefully
ease 2–4 of the slices apart and
slip in a few rosemary sprigs.
Repeat with remaining potatoes.
Brush with the oil, and season
well with salt and pepper.

2 Place the seasoned potatoes
in a large roasting pan. Add
the parsnips, carrots, and leeks to
the potatoes, and cover with a
wire rack or trivet.

3 Beat the butter and lemon
zest together and season to
taste. Smear the chicken with the
lemon butter and place on the
rack over the vegetables.

4 Roast in the preheated oven
for 1 hour, 40 minutes,
basting the chicken and
vegetables occasionally until
cooked thoroughly. The juices
should run clear when the thigh
is pierced with a skewer. Place the
cooked chicken on a warmed
serving platter, arrange the roast
vegetables around it, and serve
immediately.

FOOD FACT

Hasselback potatoes were
named after the Stockholm
restaurant of the same name.
Using chopsticks is a great
way of ensuring that you slice
just far enough through the
potatoes so that they fan out
during cooking. The potatoes
can be given an attractive
golden finish by mixing ¼ tsp.
ground turmeric or paprika
with the oil.

SPICED INDIAN ROAST POTATOES WITH CHICKEN

INGREDIENTS   Serves 4

1½ lbs. waxy potatoes, peeled and cut into large chunks
salt and freshly ground black pepper
4 tbsp. sunflower oil
8 chicken drumsticks
1 large Spanish onion, peeled and roughly chopped
3 shallots, peeled and roughly chopped

2 large garlic cloves, peeled and crushed
1 red chili
2 tsp. finely grated ginger
2 tsp. ground cumin
2 tsp. ground coriander
pinch of cayenne pepper
4 green cardamom pods, crushed
sprigs of fresh cilantro, to garnish

1 Preheat the oven to 375° F. Parboil the potatoes for 5 minutes in lightly salted, boiling water, then drain thoroughly and set aside. Heat the oil in a large skillet, add the chicken drumsticks, and cook until sealed on all sides. Set aside.

2 Add the onions and shallots to the pan, and fry for 4–5 minutes. Stir in the garlic, chili, and ginger, and cook for 1 minute, stirring constantly. Stir in the ground cumin, coriander, cayenne pepper, and cardamom, and continue to cook, stirring, for an additional minute.

3 Add the potatoes and chicken to the pan. Season to taste with salt and pepper. Stir gently until the potatoes and chicken pieces are coated in the onion and spice mixture.

4 Spoon into a large roasting pan and roast in the preheated oven for 35 minutes, or until the chicken and potatoes are cooked thoroughly. Garnish with fresh cilantro and serve immediately.

HANDY HINT

Spanish onions are the largest white onions and they have a far milder flavor than many smaller varieties. When frying onions, as in this recipe, do not be tempted to chop them in a food processor, as this will make them too wet, and, as a result, the onions will steam rather than fry.

SPECIAL RÖSTI

INGREDIENTS Serves 4

1½ lbs. potatoes, scrubbed but not peeled

salt and freshly ground black pepper

⅓ cup butter

1 large onion, peeled and finely chopped

1 garlic clove, peeled and crushed

2 tbsp. freshly chopped parsley

1 tbsp. olive oil

scant ¼ lb. prosciutto, thinly sliced

½ cup sun-dried tomatoes, chopped

1½ cups shredded Emmentaler cheese

mixed green salad, to serve

1 Cook the potatoes in a large saucepan of salted, boiling water for about 10 minutes until just tender. Drain in a colander, then rinse in cold water. Drain again. Leave until cool enough to handle, then peel off the skins.

2 Melt the butter in a large skillet and gently fry the onion and garlic for about 3 minutes until softened and beginning to color. Remove from the heat.

3 Shred the potatoes into a large bowl, then stir in the onion and garlic mixture. Sprinkle over the parsley and stir well to mix. Season to taste with salt and pepper.

4 Heat the oil in the frying pan and cover the bottom of the pan with half the potato mixture. Lay the slices of prosciutto on top. Sprinkle with the chopped sun-dried tomatoes first, then with the Emmentaler cheese.

5 Finally, top with the remaining potato mixture. Cook over a low heat, pressing down with a palette knife from time to time, for 10–15 minutes or until the bottom is golden brown. Carefully invert the rösti onto a large plate, then carefully slide it back into the pan and cook the other side until golden. Serve cut into wedges, with a mixed green salad.

HELPFUL HINT

To make sure the rösti is the right thickness, you will need a heavy-based, nonstick skillet with a diameter of about 9 in.

MEDITERRANEAN POTATO SALAD

INGREDIENTS   Serves 4

1½ lbs. small, waxy potatoes
2 red onions, peeled and
  roughly chopped
1 yellow bell pepper, deseeded
  and roughly chopped
1 green bell pepper, deseeded
  and roughly chopped
6 tbsp. extra-virgin olive oil
⅓ cup chopped ripe tomatoes
½ cup sliced, pitted black
  olives
¼ lb. feta cheese

3 tbsp. freshly chopped
  parsley
2 tbsp. white wine vinegar
1 tsp. Dijon mustard
1 tsp. honey
salt and freshly ground black
  pepper
sprigs of fresh parsley, to
  garnish

1 Preheat the oven to 400° F. Place the potatoes in a large saucepan of salted water, bring to a boil, and simmer until just tender. Do not overcook. Drain and plunge into cold water to keep them from cooking further.

2 Place the onions in a bowl with the yellow and green peppers, then pour 2 tablespoons of the olive oil over. Stir and spoon onto a large baking sheet. Cook in the preheated oven for 25–30 minutes or until the vegetables are tender and lightly charred in places, stirring occasionally. Remove from the oven and transfer to a large bowl.

3 Cut the potatoes into bite-sized pieces and mix with the roasted onions and peppers. Add the tomatoes and olives. Crumble over the feta cheese and sprinkle with the chopped parsley.

4 Whisk together the remaining olive oil, vinegar, mustard, and honey, then season to taste with salt and pepper. Pour the dressing over the potatoes and toss gently together. Garnish with parsley sprigs and serve immediately.

FOOD FACT

Tomatoes are such an integral part of many cuisines that it is hard to believe they were only introduced to Europe from the Americas a few hundred years ago. There are lots of new varieties now available to try. Those sold still attached to the vine tend to have a particularly good flavor.

POTATO & GOAT CHEESE TART

INGREDIENTS   Serves 6

10 oz. prepared basic pie
   dough, thawed if frozen
1¼ lbs. small, waxy potatoes
salt and freshly ground black
   pepper
beaten egg, for brushing
2 tbsp. sun-dried tomato paste
¼ tsp. chili powder, or to taste
1 large egg

⅔ cup sour cream
⅔ cup milk
2 tbsp. freshly cut chives
¾ lb. goat cheese, sliced
salad and warm, crusty bread,
   to serve

1 Preheat the oven to 375° F.
Roll the pastry out on a
lightly floured surface and use to
line a 9-in. fluted quiche pan.
Chill in the refrigerator for 30
minutes.

2 Scrub the potatoes, place in a
large saucepan of lightly
salted water, and bring to a boil.
Simmer for 10–15 minutes or
until the potatoes are tender.
Drain and set aside until cool
enough to handle.

3 Line the pie shell with waxed
paper and baking beans and
bake blind in the preheated oven
for 15 minutes. Remove from the
oven and discard the paper and
beans. Brush the dough with a
little beaten egg, then return to
the oven and cook for an
additional 5 minutes. Remove
from the oven.

4 Cut the potatoes into ½-in.-
thick slices; set aside. Spread
the sun-dried tomato paste over

the base of pie shell, sprinkle with
the chili powder, then arrange the
potato slices on top in a
decorative pattern.

5 Beat together the egg, sour
cream, milk, and chives, then
season to taste with salt and
pepper. Pour over the potatoes.
Arrange the goat cheese on top of
the potatoes. Bake in the preheated
oven for 30 minutes until golden
brown. Serve immediately with
salad and warm bread.

HELPFUL HINT

Using store-bought pie dough
is a good way to save time,
but always remove it from the
refrigerator 10–15 minutes
before rolling it out,
otherwise it may be difficult
to handle. Brushing the base
with egg helps seal the
dough, and keeps it crisp
when filled.

POTATO PANCAKES WITH SMOKED SALMON

INGREDIENTS   Serves 4

2⅔ cups floury potatoes, diced
salt and freshly ground black
  pepper
1 large egg
1 large egg yolk
2 tbsp. butter
¼ cup all-purpose flour
⅔ cup heavy cream
2 tbsp. freshly chopped parsley
5 tbsp. crème fraîche

1 tbsp. horseradish sauce
½ lb. smoked salmon, sliced
lettuce leaves, to serve

TO GARNISH:
lemon slices
cut chives

1 Cook the potatoes in a saucepan of lightly salted, boiling water for 15–20 minutes or until tender. Drain thoroughly, then mash until free of lumps. Beat in the whole egg and egg yolk, along with the butter. Beat until smooth and creamy. Slowly beat in the flour and cream, then season to taste with salt and pepper. Stir in the chopped parsley.

2 Beat the crème fraîche and horseradish sauce together in a small bowl, cover with plastic wrap, and set aside until needed.

3 Heat a lightly greased, heavy-based skillet over a medium-high heat. Place a few spoonfuls of the potato mixture in the hot pan, and cook for 4–5 minutes or until cooked and golden, turning halfway through cooking time. Remove from the pan, drain on paper towels, and keep warm.

Repeat with the remaining mixture.

4 Arrange the pancakes on individual serving plates. Place the smoked salmon on the pancakes, and spoon over a little of the horseradish sauce. Serve with salad and the remaining horseradish sauce, and garnish with lemon slices and chives.

TASTY TIP

Horseradish is a pungent root, usually finely grated and mixed with oil and vinegar or cream to make horseradish sauce. Commercially-made sauces vary, so it is best to add a little at a time to the cream and taste after each addition until you have the desired flavor.

SALMON WITH HERBED POTATOES

INGREDIENTS   Serves 4

1 lb. baby new potatoes
salt and freshly ground black
  pepper
4 salmon steaks, each about
  6 oz.
1 carrot, peeled and cut into
  fine strips
12 asparagus spears, trimmed
1 cup snow peas, trimmed

finely grated zest and juice 1
  lemon
2 tbsp. butter
4 large sprigs of fresh parsley

1 Preheat the oven to 375° F. Parboil the potatoes in lightly salted, boiling water for 5–8 minutes until they are barely tender. Drain and set aside.

2 Cut out 4 pieces of baking parchment, measuring 8 in. square, and place on the work surface. Arrange the parboiled potatoes on top. Wipe the salmon steaks and place on top of the potatoes.

3 Place the carrot strips in a bowl with the asparagus spears, snow peas, and grated lemon zest and juice. Season to taste with salt and pepper. Toss lightly together.

4 Divide the vegetables evenly between the salmon. Dot the top of each pocket with butter and add a sprig of parsley.

5 To wrap a pocket, lift up 2 opposite sides of the paper and fold the edges together. Twist the paper at the other 2 ends to seal the pocket well. Repeat with the remaining pockets.

6 Place the pockets on a baking sheet and bake for 15 minutes. Place an unopened pocket on each plate, and open before eating.

HELPFUL HINT

Cooking fish *en papillote* is an excellent way of keeping in all the juices, flavor, and aroma of the fish and vegetables. Your guests will also enjoy the anticipation of opening these surprise packages. Let the pockets stand for a few minutes before serving, as the steam can be burning hot when opened.

LAMB & POTATO MOUSSAKA

INGREDIENTS   Serves 4

1½ lbs. cooked roast lamb
1½ lbs. potatoes, peeled
½ cup butter
1 large onion, peeled and
　chopped
2–4 garlic cloves, peeled and
　crushed
3 tbsp. tomato paste
1 tbsp. freshly chopped parsley
salt and freshly ground black

pepper
3–4 tbsp. olive oil
2 medium eggplants, trimmed
　and sliced
4 medium tomatoes, sliced
2 medium eggs
1¼ cups plain yogurt
2–3 tbsp. grated Parmesan
　cheese

1　Preheat the oven to 400° F. Trim the lamb, discarding any fat, then dice and set aside. Thinly slice the potatoes and rinse thoroughly in cold water, then pat dry with a clean dishtowel.

2　Melt half the butter in a skillet and fry the potatoes in batches until crisp and golden. Using a slotted spoon, remove from the pan and set aside. Use a third of the potatoes to line the base of an ovenproof dish.

3　Add the onion and garlic to the butter remaining in the pan and cook for 5 minutes. Add the lamb and fry for 1 minute. Blend the tomato paste with 3 tablespoons of water and stir into the pan with the parsley and salt and pepper. Spoon over the layer of potatoes, then top with the remaining potato slices.

4　Heat the oil and the remaining butter in the pan, and brown the eggplant slices for 5–6 minutes. Arrange the tomatoes on top of the potatoes, then the eggplants on top of the tomatoes. Beat the eggs with the yogurt and Parmesan cheese, and pour over the eggplants and tomatoes. Bake in the preheated oven for 25 minutes or until golden and piping hot. Serve.

HANDY HINT

It is worth salting the eggplants to ensure that any bitterness is removed. Layer the slices in a colander, sprinkling a little salt between the layers. Leave for 20 minutes, then rinse under cold running water, and pat dry on paper towels. Salting helps the eggplants to absorb less oil when frying.

CROWN ROAST OF LAMB

INGREDIENTS

Serves 6

1 lamb crown roast
salt and freshly ground black
  pepper
1 tbsp. sunflower oil
1 small onion, peeled and
  finely chopped
2–3 garlic cloves, peeled and
  crushed
2 celery stalks, trimmed and
  finely chopped
½ cup cooked mixed basmati
  and wild rice

½ cup chopped dried apricots
⅓ cup pine nuts, toasted
1 tbsp. finely grated orange
  zest
2 tbsp. freshly chopped
  cilantro
1 small egg, beaten
freshly roasted potatoes and
  green vegetables, to serve

1 Preheat the oven to 350° F.
Wipe the crown roast, and
season the cavity with salt and
pepper. Place in a roasting pan,
and cover the ends of the bones
with small pieces of aluminum
foil.

2 Heat the oil in a small
saucepan, and cook the
onion, garlic, and celery for 5
minutes, then remove the
saucepan from the heat. Add the
cooked rice with the apricots,
pine nuts, orange zest, and
cilantro. Season with salt and
pepper, then stir in the egg and
mix well.

3 Carefully spoon the prepared
stuffing into the cavity of the
lamb, then roast in the preheated
oven for 1–1½ hours. Remove the
lamb from the oven, and remove
and discard the aluminum foil
from the bones. Return to the

oven and continue to cook for an
additional 15 minutes.

4 Remove from the oven and
let rest for 10 minutes before
serving with the roast potatoes
and freshly cooked vegetables.

FOOD FACT

The crown roast is made by
joining 2 rib joints together,
making a perfect central
cavity to fill with stuffing. For
a special occasion, when
ready to serve, the trimmed
bones may be topped with
white paper frills, like tiny
chefs' hats.

TERIYAKI BEEF

INGREDIENTS
Serves 4

1¼ lb. steak
1 medium onion, peeled and
  finely sliced
2-in. piece of ginger, peeled
  and coarsely chopped
1 bird's eye chili, deseeded
  and finely chopped
6 tbsp. light soy sauce
2 tbsp. sake or sweet sherry
1 tbsp. lemon juice

1 tsp. honey
1½ cups glutinous rice
sunflower oil, for spraying

TO GARNISH:

carrots, finely sliced
daikon, finely sliced
sprigs of fresh cilantro

1 Trim the steak, discarding any fat or gristle, and place in a shallow, nonmetallic dish. Spread the sliced onion over the steak. Mix the ginger with the chili, and sprinkle over the steak and onion.

2 Blend the soy sauce with the sake or sherry, the lemon juice, and honey. Stir well, then pour over the steak and onion. Cover and marinate in the refrigerator for at least 1 hour, longer if time permits. Turn the steak over or occasionally spoon the marinade over the meat during this time.

3 Place the rice in a saucepan with 2 cups of water and cook for 15 minutes or until tender. Drain if necessary, then pack into four warmed, greased, individual molds. Quickly invert onto four individual warm plates and keep warm.

4 Spray or brush a griddle with oil, then heat until really hot. Drain the steak and cook on the griddle for 2–3 minutes on each side, or until cooked as desired. Remove from the pan and slice thinly. Arrange on the warm serving plates, garnish with the carrots, daikon, and cilantro sprigs, then serve.

FOOD FACT

There are more than 200 different types of chilies. The heat comes from capsaicin, a compound found in the membranes and seeds, and, to a lesser extent, in the flesh. Chilies range in potency from very mild to blisteringly hot. Bird's eye chilies, whether red or green, are one of the smallest and the hottest.

INDEX